Teacher's Guide

PATHWAYS

Listening, Speaking, and Critical Thinking

2

Becky Tarver Chase
Ingrid Wisniewska

NATIONAL GEOGRAPHIC LEARNING |  **HEINLE CENGAGE Learning**

Australia • Brazil • Japan • Korea • Mexico • Singapore • Spain • United Kingdom • United States

Pathways 2 Teacher's Guide
Listening, Speaking, and Critical Thinking

Publisher: Sherrise Roehr

Executive Editor: Laura Le Dréan

Acquisitions Editor: Tom Jefferies

Development Editor: Lydia Sheldon,
Marissa Petrarca

Director of Global Marketing: Ian Martin

Marketing Manager: Caitlin Thomas

Marketing Manager: Emily Stewart

Director of Content and Media Production:
Michael Burggren

Senior Content Project Manager: Daisy Sosa

Manufacturing Manager: Marcia Locke

Manufacturing Buyer: Marybeth Hennebury

Cover Design: Page 2 LLC

Cover Image: Fred Bavendam/Minden Pictures/
National Geographic Image Collection

Interior Design: Page 2 LLC, Cenveo Publisher
Services/Nesbitt Graphics, Inc.

Composition: Cenveo Publisher Services/
Nesbitt Graphics, Inc.

ISBN-13: 978-1-111-39861-3

ISBN-10: 1-111-39861-5

National Geographic Learning
20 Channel Center St.
Boston, MA 02210
USA

Cengage Learning is a leading provider of customized learning solutions with office locations around the globe, including Singapore, the United Kingdom, Australia, Mexico, Brazil, and Japan. Locate your local office at:
international.cengage.com/region

Cengage Learning products are represented in Canada by Nelson Education, Ltd.

Visit Heinle online at **ngl.cengage.com**
Visit our corporate website at **www.cengage.com**

Printed in the United States of America
3 4 5 6 7 8 15 14 13 12

TABLE OF CONTENTS

Advantages of *Pathways Listening, Speaking, and Critical Thinking*

In *Pathways Listening, Speaking, and Critical Thinking*, real-world content from *National Geographic* publications provides a context for meaningful language acquisition. Students learn essential, high-frequency vocabulary, review important grammatical structures, and practice listening and speaking skills that will allow them to succeed in both academic and social settings.

Pathways Listening, Speaking, and Critical Thinking can be used in a wide variety of language-learning programs, from high schools and community colleges to private institutes and intensive English programs. The high-interest content motivates students and teachers alike.

The following features are included in *Pathways Listening, Speaking, and Critical Thinking*:

- Academic Pathways give students and teachers clear performance objectives for each unit.

- Opening pages introduce the unit theme and provide key vocabulary and concepts.

- Interesting content is used to present target vocabulary and to spark discussions.

- Extensive audio programs include lectures, interviews, conversations, and pronunciation models that expose students to many different kinds of speakers.

- Clear grammar charts present key grammar structures and explain language functions such as asking for clarification and sustaining a conversation.

- Presentation Skills boxes highlight skills for planning and delivering successful oral presentations.

- Student to Student boxes provide real-world expressions for making friends and working with classmates.

- An *Independent Student Handbook* and vocabulary index at the end of each level serve as tools to use in class or for self-study and review.

Teaching Language Skills and Academic Literacy

Students need more than language skills to succeed in an academic setting. In addition to teaching the English language, the *Pathways* series teaches academic literacy, which includes not only reading, writing, speaking, and listening skills, but also visual literacy, classroom participation and collaboration skills, critical thinking, and the ability to use technology for learning. Students today are expected to be motivated, inquisitive, original, and creative. In short, they're expected to possess quite an extensive skill set before they even begin their major course of study.

Using *National Geographic* Content in a Language Class

The use of high-interest content from *National Geographic* publications sets the *Pathways* series apart. Instead of working with topics that might seem irrelevant, students are engaged by fascinating stories about real people and places around the world and the issues that affect us all.

High-interest content is introduced throughout each unit—as context for target vocabulary, as content for lectures and conversation—and provides the information students need for lively discussions and interesting presentations.

The topics in the *Pathways Listening, Speaking, and Critical Thinking* series correspond to academic subject areas and appeal to a wide range of interests. For example:

Academic Subject Area	Unit Title	Unit Theme
Health Science	*Inside the Brain*	the physiology and psychology of the human brain
History/Archaeology	*Learning from the Past*	recent underwater discoveries and the lessons they impart about the value of history
Anthropology/Sociology	*Culture and Tradition*	traditions from cultures around the world, from cowboys to Caribbean music
Earth Science	*Fascinating Planet*	the geography and geology of national parks in China, Brazil, Madagascar, and New Zealand
Economics/Business	*Making a Living, Making a Difference*	economic development including cooperatives, cottage industries, entrepreneurs, and charitable organizations

Increasing Visual Literacy

Photographs, maps, charts, and graphs can all convey enormous amounts of information. Lecturers and professors rarely give oral presentations without some kind of visual aid. Helping students to make sense of visuals is an important part of preparing them for academic success.

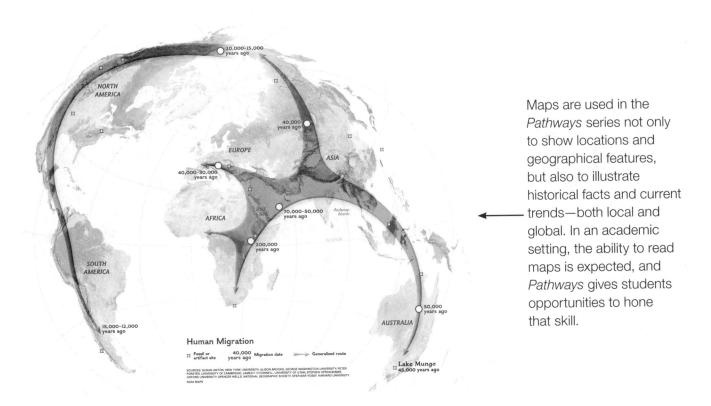

Maps are used in the *Pathways* series not only to show locations and geographical features, but also to illustrate historical facts and current trends—both local and global. In an academic setting, the ability to read maps is expected, and *Pathways* gives students opportunities to hone that skill.

Charts and graphs present numerical data in a visual way, and the *Pathways* series gives students practice in reading them. In addition to the standard pie charts and bar graphs, *Pathways* includes more unusual visuals from the pages of *National Geographic* publications.

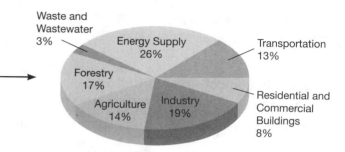

Graphic organizers have several functions in the *Pathways* series. They appeal to visual learners by showing relationships between ideas in a visual way. So, in addition to texts and listening passages, *Pathways* uses graphic organizers to present interesting content. Students are asked to use graphic organizers for a number of academic tasks such as brainstorming or organizing notes for a presentation.

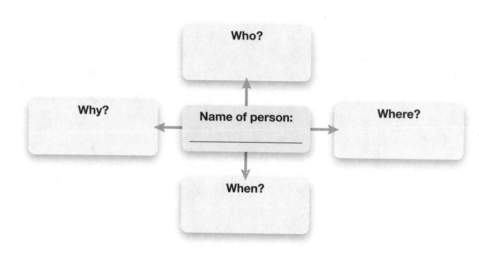

The photographs in the *Pathways* series go far beyond decorating the pages. Photographs introduce the unit theme and provide necessary background information for understanding listening passages and texts. Teachers will also want to exploit the photographs in *Pathways* to initiate discussions and reinforce the target language.

Building Critical Thinking Skills

Critical thinking skills are explicitly taught and practiced in *Pathways Listening, Speaking, and Critical Thinking*. One reason for this is that critical thinking—the ability to make judgments and decisions based on evidence and reason—is an essential skill for students in an academic setting, where they're expected to reflect on and analyze information rather than simply remember it. Students need to be prepared to think critically while listening, reading, writing, and participating in discussions. The skills of critical thinking do not develop on their own; they need to be taught, learned, and practiced.

The ability to think critically is also required in most careers, and critical thinking contributes to language acquisition by requiring deep processing of the language. In order to consider an idea in relation to other ideas and then articulate a response or an opinion about it, we must make complex associations in the brain. This, in turn, leads to better comprehension and retention of the target language.

Here are just a few examples of the academic tasks that require critical thinking skills:

- deciding which material from a lecture to take notes on
- determining a speaker's purpose when assessing the content of a talk
- forming an opinion on an issue based on facts and evidence
- relating new information to one's personal experiences
- giving specific examples to support one's main idea
- assessing the credibility of a source of information

The *Pathways* series gives explicit instruction on and practice of critical thinking skills. Each unit has a Critical Thinking Focus and several practice exercises. For example:

> ### Critical Thinking Focus: Drawing Conclusions
>
> When you draw a conclusion, you make a logical judgment about something based on the information you have. For example, *I might stop by your house. If there are no lights on, and when I knock on the door nobody answers, I'll probably conclude that nobody is home. I can't know this for certain since I can't go into the house and look around, but I do have enough information to reach a logical conclusion.*

 A | In a group, discuss the information from this unit about Angkor and the Khmer Empire and list some conclusions you can draw based on this information. Consider the topics below.

- The length of time that Angkor was the capital of the Khmer Empire
- The art and architecture that can be seen at Angkor
- The number of temples built at Angkor
- The size and sophistication of the water control systems in and around Angkor

> We can conclude that there were a lot of workers in Angkor. Somebody had to construct those huge man-made lakes.

- The fact that Angkor's wealth and power declined after losing river access to the sea
- The fact that Angkor Wat is on UNESCO's World Heritage site list

Teaching with *Pathways Listening, Speaking, and Critical Thinking*

Using the Opening Pages

Each unit of *Pathways Listening, Speaking, and Critical Thinking* begins with a unit opener and a two-page spread called Exploring the Theme. These opening pages serve the important functions of raising student interest in the unit theme and introducing key vocabulary and concepts.

The Unit Opener

Every unit opener features a stunning photograph that draws students into the unit theme. You'll want to direct students' attention to the photograph and the unit title. Give students a chance to react to the photograph and give the class some of the background information that you'll find in the Teacher's Guide.

Every unit opener also includes Think and Discuss questions that encourage students to interact with the photograph and to relate it to their own lives.

The unit opener also lists the Academic Pathways for each unit. These are clearly-stated performance objectives that preview some of the main culminating activities in the unit. The Academic Pathways are also useful in assessing students' progress at the end of each unit.

Exploring the Theme

After you've worked with the unit opener, go on to the two-page Exploring the Theme section, which provides information in the form of maps, captioned photographs, charts and graphs, and short articles. This section gives students the background information and key terms they need before beginning the unit.

The Exploring the Theme questions check students' comprehension of the information and give them a chance to respond to it in a meaningful way.

Building Vocabulary

Each level of *Pathways Listening, Speaking, and Critical Thinking* contains approximately 200 target vocabulary words in addition to footnotes for less frequently used words. The target vocabulary words in the *Pathways* series are . . .

- **High-frequency:** Students are likely to use high-frequency words on a regular basis, which leads to greater acquisition and better fluency.

- **Level-appropriate:** The target vocabulary words in each level of the *Pathways* series are appropriate for the students studying in that level.

- **Useful for discussing the unit theme:** The vocabulary words in each unit are introduced in the vocabulary sections, used in the listening passages, and recycled in many of the activities.

- **Informed by the Academic Word List:** The *Pathways* series contains a high percentage of the words found on the Academic Word List*.

*The Academic Word List (AWL) is a list of the 570 highest-frequency academic word families that regularly appear in academic texts. The AWL was compiled by researcher Averil Coxhead based on her analysis of a 3.5-million-word corpus (Coxhead, 2000).

Developing Listening Skills

Each unit of *Pathways Listening, Speaking, and Critical Thinking* contains two listening sections. The listening passage in Lesson A takes place in a relatively formal context such as a lecture, a meeting, or a formal presentation. Lesson B presents an informal speaking situation such as a conversation between friends or a group project with classmates.

The language in the listening passages represents realistic situations, yet the language is controlled for level, and students may listen to each passage more than once. This guided listening gives students the chance to practice listening and note-taking skills and to develop the confidence and fluency they'll need before they are immersed in an academic setting.

Each listening section contains three parts:

- **Before Listening** activities provide background information and explicit instruction in listening skills.
- **While Listening** activities give students practice in listening for main ideas, listening for smaller details, and in making inferences.
- **After Listening** activities are designed to reinforce listening skills and to allow students to discuss and react to the listening passage.

Pronunciation

The pronunciation lessons are designed to increase students' listening comprehension as well as the comprehensibility of their own speech. The focus is on supra-segmentals, such as rhythm and intonation patterns, rather than on individual sounds.

Note-Taking

Pathways Listening, Speaking, and Critical Thinking takes a scaffolding approach to building note-taking skills. Students begin by listening for specific information to fill in blanks. Later they complete partial notes and practice independent note-taking.

Listening Critically

Since critical thinking is an essential part of listening, skills such as identifying a speaker's purpose and summarizing the main points from a talk are part of the *Pathways* listening program.

Listening Homework

Extensive listening can play an important role in increasing listening comprehension. Students can expand on the listening they do in class by using the Audio CD, the Online Workbook, and the Presentation Tool CD-ROM.

Developing Speaking Skills

Every section of *Pathways Listening, Speaking, and Critical Thinking* provides opportunities for classroom speaking and discussion, often in pairs or in small groups. The Exploring Spoken English sections focus entirely on speaking. Striking images and brief stories about real people and places often provide the content for engaging interactions.

Accurate Speech

Clear and succinct grammar lessons give students a single language structure to concentrate on for each Exploring Spoken English section. The grammar points lend themselves to discussion of the unit theme and can be recycled throughout the unit.

Fluent Speech

Frequent classroom discussions and interactions prepare students to participate in class and succeed in an academic setting. Language Function boxes address the situations in which stock expressions or target grammatical structures are commonly used, increasing the students' level of comfort and confidence in dealing with common speaking situations.

Speaking activities are designed with a scaffolding approach. They progress from controlled activities to guided activities and free activities. Early confidence-building motivates students to attempt activities that increase in difficulty, taking them to their ultimate goal—participation in authentic speaking activities such as classroom presentations, formal discussions, and debates.

Presentation Skills boxes appear at points where students give presentations, so they provide immediate practice of skills needed for planning and delivering successful oral presentations.

Student to Student boxes provide tips and expressions to help students develop the informal, one-on-one speaking skills they will need for class work and in their day-to-day exchanges.

Engage is a consolidating speaking activity. It is a task or project involving collaboration with a partner or a group as well as an oral presentation of results or ideas.

Using Videos in the Language Classroom

The video clips in *Pathways Listening, Speaking, and Critical Thinking* come from the award-winning *National Geographic* film collection and act as a bridge between Lesson A and Lesson B of each unit. The videos consolidate content and skills from Lesson A and illustrate a specific aspect of the unit theme in a visually dynamic way.

What is the Lesson A and B Viewing section?

The Viewing section features a video on a theme related to the whole unit. All video clips are on the Online Workbook, the Presentation Tool CD-ROM, as well as on the classroom DVD.

Why teach video-viewing skills?

In daily life, non-fiction videos can be found on television, on the Internet, and in movie theaters in the form of documentaries. Just as *Pathways* provides a wide variety of listening passages to build students' listening skills, the series also builds viewing skills with videos from *National Geographic*. *Pathways* promotes visual and digital literacy so learners can competently use a wide range of modern media.

Videos differ from listening texts in important ways. First, students are processing information by viewing and listening simultaneously. Visual images include information about the video's setting as well as clues found in nonverbal communication, such as facial expressions and body movements. The video may also include animated maps and diagrams to explain information and processes. The soundtrack contains narration, conversations, music, and sound effects. Some contextual words may appear on screen in signs or as identification of people or settings. In addition, full English subtitles (closed captions) are available as a teaching and learning option.

What are the stages of viewing?

Before Viewing prepares students for the video, engages their background knowledge about the topic, and creates interest in what they will watch. Effective ways of previewing the video include:

- brainstorming about and discussing what the class already knows about the topic;
- using photographs and the video's title to predict the content;
- pre-teaching key vocabulary essential to understanding the video content;
- and skimming the summary reading.

While Viewing may occur multiple times and at different speeds while:

- picking out and understanding the main ideas of the video;
- watching and listening closely for detail;
- and watching and listening for opinion and inference.

After Viewing activities include:

- describing the main points and the sequence of events in the video;
- completing the cloze summary with provided target vocabulary;
- and answering discussion questions that relate the video to students' own lives or experiences.

How should teachers use the videos to teach?

The narration on each video has been carefully graded to feature vocabulary items and structures that are appropriate for students' proficiency level. Here are techniques for using video in class:

- Have students preview the video by reading the transcript or the summary paragraph.
- Pause, rewind, or fast-forward the video to focus on key segments or events.
- Pause the video midway to allow students to predict what will happen next. Resume the video so students can check their predictions.
- Have students watch the video with the sound off so they can focus only on what they see. If this approach is used, follow-up discussion helps students share their ideas about the content of the video. Then play the video with the sound on for students to check their ideas.
- Have students watch without subtitles after which they discuss what they see then play with subtitles for students to check their ideas.
- Have students follow the script as they listen to the video to help with intonation, pitch, and stress. Stop and replay key phrases for students to repeat.
- Have students watch the video independently and complete the comprehension questions on the Online Workbook.
- To extend viewing skills to speaking and writing skills, have students make a presentation or create a written report about a video of their choice, using language they have learned from the Student Book and video narration.

All video scripts are found at the back of the Teacher's Guide. Teachers have flexibility in how or whether they want students to use the scripts. See individual units in this Teacher's Guide for specific teaching suggestions for each video.

Features of the *Pathways* Teacher's Guide

The *Pathways* Teacher's Guide contains teaching notes, answer keys, and the audio and video scripts. There are also warm-up activities to help teachers present the material in the textbook and overviews of the unit theme and the video clip to help turn teachers into "instant experts."

Academic Pathways Boxes

Each unit in the Teacher's Guide begins with a preview of the Academic Pathways. A description of each pathway is then given at the point where it occurs in the unit along with helpful information for the teacher. Teachers are also directed to the online and Assessment CD-ROM with Exam*View*® resources that will help to reinforce and assess the skills learned for each Academic Pathway.

Ideas for... Boxes

Throughout the *Pathways* Teacher's Guide, you will find boxes with ideas to help both novice and experienced teachers. There are four types of Ideas for... boxes:

- **Ideas for Presenting Grammar** boxes provide a variety of ways to introduce grammatical structures and utilize the grammar charts.

- **Ideas for Checking Comprehension** boxes remind teachers of the need to continually assess students' comprehension during every class session.

- **Ideas for Expansion** boxes suggest ways to expand on the content of the book when students need extra instruction or when they have a high level of interest in a topic.

- **Ideas for Multi-level Classes** boxes provide techniques to use in mixed-ability classrooms, where learner diversity can benefit everyone in the class. On the other hand, providing the right kind of help for all the students in any classroom can be a balancing act. When different types of instruction are needed for different learners, teachers must be careful not to embarrass lower-level learners in any way or detract from the learning experience of higher-level learners.

Tips

Tips for instruction and classroom management are provided throughout the *Pathways* Teacher's Guide. The tips are especially helpful to less experienced teachers, but they are also a resource for more experienced teachers, providing new ideas and adding variety to the classroom routine.

Staying Healthy in the Modern World

Academic Track
Health Science

Academic Pathways:
Lesson A: Listening to a Talk about Preventing Heart Disease
Giving a Presentation on Health and Exercise Habits
Lesson B: Listening to an Informal Conversation
Keeping a Conversation Going

Unit Theme

Staying healthy is important to everyone, regardless of age.

Unit 1 explores the topic of health as it relates to:
– life expectancy
– heart disease
– exercise
– allergies

Think and Discuss *(page 1)*

5 mins

- Ask students to describe the photo. Ask them what the man is doing. (*He's standing on his head. / He's doing a headstand.*)

- Brainstorm ideas for why he is doing this (e.g., *health, exercise, meditation, relaxation*).

- Ask for students' reactions to the photo. What is surprising or interesting about the photo?

Exploring the Theme: Staying Healthy in the Modern World *(pages 2-3)*

15 mins

The opening spread features a busy scene in a densely populated city.

- Ask students to describe the scene and write possible adjectives on the board, such as *crowded, polluted, noisy,* and *stressful.*

- Discuss the advantages and disadvantages of living in a large city. Make a list of them on the board.

- Discuss the possible negative health effects of living in a large city such as this one. Ask what can be done to counteract the negative health effects.

- Look at the three photos and read the captions.

- Brainstorm other ideas to reduce stress, exercise regularly, and eat a healthy diet.

- Read the three questions on page 2 and ask students to write their answers in class or in their journals for homework.

> **IDEAS FOR... Expansion**
>
> Ask students to imagine the life of a person in this city and write a short description of what it feels like from his or her point of view.

Building and Using Vocabulary (pages 4-5)

30 mins

WARM-UP

The Lesson A target vocabulary is presented in the context of living a long life.

- Ask students to give some advice on how to stay healthy.
- Discuss what aspects of life in your town or region are unhealthy and why.

Building Vocabulary

track 1-2

Exercise A. | Meaning from Context

- Ask students to describe the photo of the shepherd and the elderly woman. Who are these people and where are they? What do students know about these places?
- Ask students to predict what the text may say about secrets to a long life. Write all their ideas on the board in note form.
- Have students read and listen to the text. Check off which ideas they predicted correctly.
- Ask students which facts they found most interesting or surprising.

> **IDEAS FOR...   Checking Comprehension**
>
> Help students summarize the main ideas in the text by asking them to complete these sentences:
>
> *In Sardinia, men live longer because . . .*
> *In Okinawa, people live longer because . . .*

Exercise B. | Remind students to use the context to work out the meanings of the new words.

Answer Key

1. stress	**5.** diseases	**9.** diet
2. strong	**6.** cause	**10.** exercise
3. likely	**7.** pressure	
4. habit	**8.** healthy	

Using Vocabulary

Exercise A.

- Do the first item as an example.
- Allow time for students to complete their answers individually.
- Check the answers as a class.
- Note that in item 2, *exercise* is used as noun, while on page 4 it is a verb. In item 9, *disease* is singular, whereas the plural form is used on page 4.

Answer Key

1. healthy	**5.** strong	**9.** disease
2. exercise	**6.** diet	**10.** pressure
3. likely	**7.** cause	
4. stress	**8.** habit	

> **TIP**   As a follow-up, ask students to write their own sentences with blanks to test each other on the new vocabulary items. Write the best sentences on the board.

Exercise B. | Discussion

- Put students into small groups.
- Allow students time to talk about their answers in groups before discussing their ideas as a class.

Exercise C.

- Have students interview each other in pairs.
- Discuss the answer at the bottom of the page and find out who in the class is most likely to live to 100.
- Ask students if they would like to live to 100. Have them explain why or why not.

> **TIP**   At the beginning of a course, it's important that students get to know each other. Have students change partners often so that they work with different classmates.

Pronunciation Note
Ikigai: ih-**key**-guy

Developing Listening Skills

(pages 6-7)

Pronunciation: Word Endings -s and -es

 Exercise A.
track 1-3
track 1-4

- Ask students to circle all -s and -es word endings on nouns and verbs in the two sentences.

- Play the audio. Ask students if they can work out the rule for -s and -es endings.

- Read the rule and the examples together.

- Play the audio and ask students to repeat the words.

 Exercise B.
track 1-5

- Ask students to look at the photo and describe what is happening. (*A nurse is serving food to an elderly patient.*)

- Play the audio while students underline the -s and -es word endings.

- Compare answers as a class.

Answer Key thanks, nurses (2x), minutes

Exercise C. | Have students work in pairs and take turns reading the text aloud. Challenge them to think of new sentences using these words.

Before Listening

Exercise A. | Prior Knowledge Ask students to take out their vocabulary journals. They may want to use their dictionaries to check the meanings of these words.

Exercise B. | Predicting Content

- Ask students what they already know about preventing heart disease.

- Discuss which words will probably occur in the talk.

Listening: A Talk about Preventing Heart Disease

 Exercise A.
track 1-6

- Play the audio. Have students check their answers to the previous exercise (Predicting Content).

 Exercise B. | Listening for Main Ideas
track 1-6

- Play the audio again.

- Ask students what the three main topics are.

Answer Key

1. Get your blood pressure checked., Eat less salt and sugar., Get enough exercise., Visit your doctor.

2. high blood pressure, high blood sugar, smoking

Exercise C. | Listening for Details Play the audio again as students listen and choose the correct answer.
track 1-6

Answer Key   1. a 2. b 3. b

IDEAS FOR... Checking Comprehension

Ask these additional questions orally or write them on the board.

1. What is Tara Sorenson's job? (*She's a public health nurse.*)

2. What type of heart disease does she talk about? (*coronary*)

3. Why is high blood pressure dangerous? (*It can enlarge and weaken the heart. It can damage the blood vessels, which means the blood vessels are unable to bring enough blood and oxygen to the heart. This lack of blood and oxygen causes a heart attack.*)

After Listening

Critical Thinking | Critical thinking questions encourage students to apply higher-order thinking skills to a topic. Here, students evaluate the information and relate it to their own lives.

IDEAS FOR... Expansion

Students can work in groups to develop a questionnaire to find out how healthily their classmates live. They can use their questionnaire to carry out a class survey.

Exploring Spoken English

45 mins *(pages 8-10)*

Grammar: Adverbs of Frequency

track 1-7 **Exercise A. | Prior Knowledge**

- Briefly discuss the photo and ask students what they think an experienced cyclist would normally do to prepare for a bike trip.

- Play the audio and ask students what type of words the underlined words are. (*adverbs of frequency*)

- Look at the chart and read the rules.

IDEAS FOR... Presenting Grammar

- To practice word order as well as the meaning of these adverbs of frequency, read aloud some sentences without adverbs of frequency and ask students to write them down with an adverb of their choice so that the sentences are true about them.

  I play soccer.
  I go running in the park.
  I am too tired to exercise.
  I am too busy to go to the gym.

- Then ask students to read aloud their sentences and check if the word order is correct.

Exercise B. | Allow a few minutes for students to write their answers. Then check answers as a class by asking volunteers to read them aloud.

Answer Key

2. Kim always plays golf on Saturdays.

3. Luigi doesn't often play football.

4. I sometimes play basketball.

5. Amy usually goes swimming on the weekend. / On the weekend, Amy usually goes swimming.

6. We often do yoga.

Exercise C. | Self-Reflection Set a time limit for students to complete the sentences. After partners have compared answers, encourage them to continue the conversation by asking further questions.

TIP Encourage students to correct their own mistakes by writing their sentences from exercise C on the board and asking the class to correct them.

Language Function: Using Expressions of Frequency

- Read the language in the box.

- Have students make examples about their own lives using these expressions.

IDEAS FOR... Expansion

Make sentences about yourself and have students make corresponding sentences using the language in the box. For example:

T: *I go to the dentist in June and December.*
S: *You go to the dentist twice a year.*

Exercise A. | Critical Thinking

- Look at the photo and ask students to think of some questions to ask this person. For example: *Where do you work? What do you teach? What advice do you give to your students about diet and stress?*

Exercise B. | Collaboration

- Have students work in pairs to develop their ideas. Then ask one of the students in each pair to present their ideas to the class.

Exercise C. | Note-Taking

- Demonstrate how to take notes by asking a volunteer a question about his or her routines or habits.

TIP Have students work in different groups for this exercise. Alternatively, depending on the size of your class, this activity could be done as a class survey, with every student asking every other student about their exercise routines as they walk around the classroom.

Exercise D. | Presentation Ask each student to report about one of the other students in their group.

Speaking *(page 11)*

Giving a Presentation on Health and Exercise Habits

Exercise A. | Self-Reflection

- Give students time to answer the questions. Then have a brief class discussion of these topics.

Exercise B. | Planning a Presentation

- Go through the parts of a presentation and discuss what information could be found in each section.

- Remind students to make notes at this stage, not full sentences.

Exercise C.

track 1-8

- Explain that students will have to write the correct numbers from exercise **B** next to each paragraph and that one number is used twice.

- Play the audio and check students' answers.

> **Answer Key**   1, 2, 2, 3, 4

Exercise D.

- Read the information in the Presentation Skills box.

- Demonstrate the difference between reading from your notes and just glancing at your notes occasionally while you are speaking.

- While students are practicing, walk around the classroom and offer help and advice as needed.

Exercise E. | Presentation

- Invite students to come to the front of the class and give their presentation.

- Invite students to evaluate each other on their organization of ideas and use of notes while speaking.

- **Optional:** Record the presentations using an audio or video recorder. Then play the recording for the class and ask the class for positive comments and suggestions for improvement.

> **TIP** Since giving a presentation can be quite intimidating for students, it may be a good idea to have students give their presentation to smaller groups before they give them to the whole class.

Viewing: Bee Therapy
(pages 12-13)

30 mins

Overview of the Video | Although at first bee sting therapy sounds painful and unpleasant, some people have found it to have a positive effect on illnesses that cannot be cured by scientific medicine.

Before Viewing

Exercise A. | Discussion

- Ask students to look at the photo and tell what they know about bees.

- Ask them to predict what kind of therapy will be discussed in the video.

- Ask students to tell how they feel about modern medicine versus traditional medicine.

Exercise B. | Using a Dictionary

- Ask students to tell you which words they already know. Ask them what kinds of contexts they have heard them used in.

- Allow time for students to use their dictionaries to find the answers.

Answer Key   1. c 2. d 3. e 4. b 5. a

Exercise C. | Prior Knowledge

- Ask students to read the information and ask questions about these diseases.

- Make a list on the board of some questions that students would like to know the answers to concerning these diseases.

While Viewing

Exercise A.
4:30

- Look at the photo and ask students to describe what acupuncture is and how it works.

- Give students time to read through the questions before watching the video. Make sure students know what type of information is required. Point out

that only Mr. Chen and Mr. Chen's wife are related, even though all three people have the same name.

- Play the video and have students compare answers.

- Go over the answers as a class.

Answer Key   a. 3 b. 2 c. 1

Exercise B.
4:30

- Play the video again.

- Pause after the relevant segments if necessary.

- Go over the answers as a class.

Answer Key   1. 200, 6000 2. 600, five 3. 5000 4. three 5. six

---

IDEAS FOR...   Checking Comprehension

Play the video again and ask students to work in groups to write questions about the video. You can give each group a different section of the video. Afterwards, you may organize a competition where teams try to answer each other's questions.

After Viewing

Exercise A. | Discussion   Ask students to give their own examples to illustrate these expressions.

Answer Key   1. c 2. a 3. b

Exercise B. | Critical Thinking   If you have enough class time, ask each group to choose one person to be their spokesperson. Then, after the discussion, each spokesperson can share their group's ideas with the class.

Building and Using Vocabulary *(pages 14-15)*

WARM-UP

The Lesson B target vocabulary is presented in the context of allergies. Ask students what they know about allergies, if any of them suffer from allergies, what causes allergies, what the symptoms are, and how they can be treated.

Building Vocabulary

Exercise A. | Meaning from Context

track 1-9

- Look at the diagram.
- Ask students to try and describe the diagram first before reading the text.
- Play the audio while students read.
- Ask students to describe the diagram again after having read the text.

Exercise B.

- Encourage students to use the context to work out the meanings of each word.
- Check the meanings of any additional new vocabulary items such as *pollen, immune system, antibodies, sneezing,* and *itching.*

Answer Key
1. cell 2. enters 3. produces
4. responds 5. defends 6. occurs

IDEAS FOR...   Checking Comprehension

Make some true and false statements about the text. Have students correct the false statements. For example:

T: Pollen enters your body through your mouth.
S1: False. It enters through your nose!
T: The body's immune system thinks that the pollen is harmful.
S2: True.

Using Vocabulary

Exercise C. | Meaning from Context

track 1-10

- Read the title and ask students to predict what this text is going to be about. Ask students if they think it is going to say that hygiene helps to avoid allergies, or not.
- Pre-teach the word *hygiene* if it is unfamiliar.
- Check comprehension by asking students to summarize the text in one or two sentences.

Exercise D. | After checking students' answers, ask students to make up their own sentences and write them in their vocabulary notebooks.

Answer Key
1. contains 2. common
3. research 4. theory

Exercise E.

- Set a time limit for students to complete their sentences.
- Remind students to use the correct form of each word.
- Ask volunteers to read their sentences aloud.

Answer Key

1. enters	5. produces	9. common
2. cells	6. contains	10. responds
3. theory	7. defends	
4. occurs	8. research	

IDEAS FOR...   Expansion

Since all of these words have been previously presented in this unit, you can ask students to cover the word box with a piece of paper or a book and try to complete the sentences without looking at the words. Then have students compare their answers with the words in the box. Discuss possible alternative answers with the class.

Pronunciation Note
sclerosis: skli-**roh**-sis

Developing Listening Skills

(pages 16-17)

45 mins

Before Listening

Discussion

- Ask two students to read the conversation in the box aloud.

- Ask for their comments and opinions on the topic.

Listening: An Informal Conversation

track 1-11

Exercise A. | Listening for Main Ideas

- Explain that you will play the audio once for students to get the general idea of the conversation.

- Point out that students should identify which topic speakers are *most* concerned about (not which topics are mentioned).

> **Answer Key**   peanuts

TIP   **Allow time for students to read the questions before they listen for the answers.**

track 1-11

Exercise B. | Listening for Details

- Read the questions aloud and ask if students can answer any of them before playing the audio again.

- Go over the answers as a class.

- Note that question 1 has several possible answers.

> **Answer Key**
>
> 1. air pollution / smoke / cats / some kinds of flowers
> 2. six percent
> 3. food allergies
> 4. peanuts
> 5. between 1997 and 2002

> **IDEAS FOR...**   **Checking Comprehension**
>
> Ask some additional questions about the listening.
>
> 1. What things can cause allergies, according to Elena? (*dust and pollen*)
>
> 2. Why is air pollution bad for her? (*because she has asthma*)
>
> 3. Which foods is Elena allergic to? (*chocolate, strawberries, and peanuts*)
>
> 4. What percentage of children have food allergies nowadays? (*six percent*)

After Listening

Critical Thinking Focus: Supporting a Statement |
Read the information in the box. Discuss the differences among these three different kinds of evidence—numbers and statistics, experts, and images.

Exercise A. | Critical Thinking

- Discuss why it is important in academic writing or presentation to give supporting information.

Exercise B.

- Allow time for students to write their answers.

> **Answer Key**   *(Answers will vary.)*

Exercise C. | Critical Thinking

- Put students into groups to discuss their sentences.

- Ask volunteers to read their sentences aloud.

Exercise D. | Discussion

- Discuss the picture and the caption.

> **IDEAS FOR...**   **Expansion**
>
> Ask students to choose another health issue that they think is becoming more serious nowadays. Have them work in groups to make a list of evidence that supports the idea that their health issue has become more serious. Ask a spokesperson from each group to say what their health issue is and to read their list of evidence aloud.

Exploring Spoken English

30 mins

(pages 18-19)

Grammar: Tag Questions

- Read the information in the box and demonstrate the difference between rising and falling intonation for tag questions.

- If necessary, show students how to form tag questions. Ask students to look at the examples and work out which verb is repeated in the tag question.

track 1-12

Exercise A. | Allow time for students to complete their answers. Then play the audio.

> **Answer Key**
>
> **1.** didn't he **2.** aren't they **3.** didn't you **4.** doesn't she **5.** isn't he **6.** isn't he

track 1-12

Exercise B.

- Play the audio again and ask students to identify whether the speaker is not sure or already knows the answer.

> **Answer Key**   **1.** AK **2.** AK **3.** NS **4.** NS **5.** NS **6.** AK

Exercise C.

- Give examples of something you know about the class and something you don't know. Make sentences with tag questions and write them on the board.

- Say each question twice—once with falling intonation and once with rising intonation. Ask students which type of intonation is correct.

- Allow time for students to write their tag questions.

- Walk around the classroom, checking students' intonation as they ask and answer their questions.

> **TIP**   Ask one or two students to read their questions aloud and ask the rest of the class to identify the intonation pattern and say whether the student expects agreement or isn't sure.

Language Focus: Making Small Talk

Read the information in the box. Ask for additional suggestions for good topics for small talk.

Exercise A.

- Have students work in pairs to practice the conversations.

- Walk around the classroom to monitor students' intonation.

- Invite volunteers to read the conversations to the class.

Exercise B. | Have students work with different partners to practice small talk and tag questions.

> **IDEAS FOR... Expansion**
>
> Ask students to imagine that they are at a party. Play some soft music and ask students to walk around the classroom. When you stop the music, they have to start a conversation with someone near them using small talk and tag questions. When you start the music again, they start walking again until the music stops and they have a new conversation partner.

Engage: Keeping a Conversation Going *(page 20)*

45 mins

WARM-UP

- Discuss different strategies for keeping a conversation going.

- Discuss why this skill is important in social and business situations.

- Ask for some suggestions for how to continue a conversation, such as the ones below, and write them on the board.

A: Do you like baseball?

B: Yes.

A: _____

Or:

A: I went to a baseball game yesterday.

B: _____

Exercise A.

- Ask volunteers to read the information in the box aloud.

- Elicit another example or two for each strategy.

Exercise B. | Discussion

- Have students work in pairs. Encourage them to keep their conversations going for as long as possible.

- Remind students to use the conversational strategies above.

IDEAS FOR... Expansion

Make a list of useful words from this unit on the board for reference as students are having their conversations.

- Encourage students to use this opportunity to recycle the vocabulary they have learned in this unit.

 TIP You can repeat exercise B by having students switch partners several times.

Student to Student: Asking about Personal Knowledge and Experience | Explain that talking about personal experience is one way of supporting an opinion or an argument. Asking others about their experiences also shows that you are interested and want to learn more about them.

Exercise C.

- Read the instructions aloud.

- Put students into groups and ask group members to choose a timekeeper.

- Set a time limit for the competition.

- When they have finished, have students switch roles so that everyone gets a turn as timekeeper.

TIP Ask students to record one of their conversations and transcribe it for homework. This can be useful material for grammar or vocabulary work in your next lesson.

IDEAS FOR... Expansion

Give each student a strip of paper with a statement on it. Play music or give a signal to show that students should walk around the classroom. When you stop the music or say "Stop," students should say their statement to the nearest person. The partner will respond to the statement using the conversational strategies in this lesson and will try to continue the conversation until you say "Stop" or start the music again.

Possible statements:

I'm very interested in traditional medicine.

I've been a vegetarian for many years.

I don't believe in alternative medicines.

I think people should be more conscious about heart health.

Energy and Our Planet

Academic Track
Interdisciplinary

Academic Pathways:
Lesson A: Listening to a PowerPoint Lecture
Discussing Personal Energy Use
Lesson B: Listening to an Informal Discussion
Planning a Group Presentation

Unit Theme

Energy is an issue that many countries are dealing with nowadays. Although energy is necessary for development, the use of fossil fuels is causing many problems.

Unit 2 explores the topic of energy as it relates to:
– global warming
– personal energy use
– alternative energy
– saving energy

Think and Discuss *(page 21)*

5 ins

- Ask students to describe the photo. Why are the parts of the house in different colors? (*They show how heat is distributed.*) Which part is the hottest? (*under the roof*)

- Brainstorm ideas for how to make heating a house more efficient.

- Ask students to describe heating and energy use in their homes. What do they think they spend most energy on?

Exploring the Theme: Energy and Our Planet *(pages 22–23)*

15 ins

The opening spread features an aerial photo of London at night.

- Ask students to describe what they can see in the photo. (*the River Thames, bridges, office buildings, traffic*, etc.)

- Brainstorm adjectives to describe the scene. Ask students how cities at night are different from in the day.

Exercise A.

- Look at the two photos in the top right corner of page 23. Discuss students' responses to them. What questions do they raise about our planet and our use of the Earth's resources?

- Explain the difference between renewable and non-renewable energy sources. Ask students to think of other examples for each category.

Exercise B.

- Look at the diagrams and help students to interpret them by asking questions about them. What does each pie chart represent? What does each section represent? Does it show the amount of energy we use, or the amount we make? Has the amount increased? By how much? Why do you think this is? (*population growth, increasing industrialization, urbanization*, etc.)

- Explain the meaning of any words students ask about.

> **IDEAS FOR...** **Expansion**
>
> Ask students to work in groups to make a list of things they would like to learn about energy use or production.

Building and Using Vocabulary *(pages 24-25)*

30 mins

WARM-UP

The Lesson A target vocabulary is presented in the context of causes of global warming.

- Ask students to suggest some reasons for global warming.

- Discuss some of the reasons why we need to use energy.

Building Vocabulary

track 1-13

Exercise A. | Meaning from Context

- Ask students to look at the pictures. What other ways do we use energy in the home? What other ways does industry use energy?

- Have students read and listen to the text.

- Ask students which facts they found most interesting or surprising.

Exercise B. | Remind students to use the context to work out the meaning of the words in blue. Encourage them to think of alternative words for these vocabulary items before looking at the list.

Answer Key

1. reduce	5. impact	9. efficient
2. energy	6. increases	10. conserve
3. demand	7. significantly	
4. carbon	8. atmosphere	

Using Vocabulary

Exercise A.

- Look at the diagram and the color key with students. Ask them what they think the diagram illustrates. (*amounts of greenhouse gases emitted by different countries*)

- Explain that greenhouse gases such as carbon dioxide prevent heat from escaping Earth's atmosphere.

- Do the first item as an example. (If students ask, carbon itself is not a gas; the gas is carbon dioxide.)

- Allow time for students to complete their answers individually.

- Go over the answers as a class.

Answer Key

1. carbon	5. demand	9. efficient
2. atmosphere	6. increases	10. impact
3. significantly	7. reduce	
4. energy	8. conserve	

TIP To check comprehension, ask students to make up some questions about the text to ask each other.

Exercise B. | Understanding Visuals

- Put students into pairs.

- Allow students time to discuss their answers with their partners before gathering ideas as a class.

Developing Listening Skills
(pages 26-27)

 track 1-14
track 1-15
Pronunciation: Stressing Key Words

- Go over the information in the box.

- Play the audio. Ask students to notice the words that sound louder or stronger.

- Ask students to read Katelyn and Dan's conversation aloud in pairs and try to predict which words will be stressed.

- Play the audio and have students compare answers.

- Have students practice in pairs.

Answer Key

Students should underline the following words:
Katelyn: Environmental Club meeting
Dan: Maybe, What, about
Katelyn: presentation, energy, world, photographer, families, live
Dan: interesting, time, meeting
Katelyn: seven
Dan: science building
Katelyn: Student Union

Before Listening

Prior Knowledge | If possible, use a world map to show where these places are located.

Answer Key   a. Africa b. USA c. India

Listening: A PowerPoint Lecture

 track 1-16
Exercise A. | Listening for Main Ideas

- Look at the photos and ask students to describe what these people are doing.

- Play the audio and check the answers as a class.

Answer Key

The Panchal family, **3,** India
The Chuma family, **1,** Botswana
The Nelson family, **2,** USA

 track 1-16
Exercise B. | Listening for Details

- Play the audio again while students complete the chart with words from the lecture.

- Have students compare answers with each other before playing the audio again.

> **TIP**   While students are comparing answers, you can walk around the classroom and monitor their work to see if they need to listen to the audio one more time.

Answer Key *(Student notes may vary.)*

The Chuma family: clothes, walk, boat, electricity, a fairly small, water
The Nelson family: a machine, drive, about a gallon, more efficient, a lot of
The Panchal family: washing machine, room, bus, buy a car, million

---

IDEAS FOR...   Checking Comprehension

Ask these additional questions orally or write them on the board.

1. Who sometimes travels by boat? (*the Chuma children*)
2. Which family wants a solar-energy system? (*the Nelson family*)
3. Why do the Nelsons drive their children to school? (*because there isn't a bus*)
4. Who works in a hotel? (*Neetu Panchal's sister, Lalita*)
5. How many people live in the Panchal family's home? (*11*)
6. Which family is most impacted by global warming? (*the Panchal family*)

After Listening

Critical Thinking | Students can work in groups to develop their ideas and present them to the rest of the class when they are finished.

Pronunciation Note
Jaipur: **jahy**-poor

45 mins

Exploring Spoken English
(pages 28-30)

Language Function

Giving Examples

Read the information in the box. Give some further examples for students to complete.

Solar energy is an example of . . . *(renewable energy)*.

Many people are trying to use less fossil fuel. For example, . . . *(they ride a bike to work)*.

Exercise A. | Read the sentences in exercise **A** and go over the answers as a class.

Answer Key

2. the Chuma family is an example of this

3. For example, they bought more efficient appliances.

4. For instance, by 2050, India will have more than 600 million cars.

Exercise B. | Discuss the questions in exercise **B**.

Answer Key

1. For example, For instance
2. is an example of this
3. such as
4. for example, for instance,

Exercise C.

- Write the underlined words on the board and ask students to think of several examples for each one.

- Set a time limit for students to write their answers.

- Ask volunteers to read their sentences out loud.

Answer Key *(Answers may vary.)*

Possible answers:

1. **For example, / For instance,** I watch baseball in summer and football in winter.

   I watch sports **such as** baseball or football almost every weekend.

2. **For example, / For instance,** she studied the life cycles of elephants and lions.

   Elephants and lions **are two examples** of animal species that she has studied.

3. **For example, / For instance,** I travel to work by bus or train whenever I can.

   We can use public transportation **such as** bus or train to save energy.

4. **For example, / For instance,** coal and gas produce a lot of carbon dioxide.

   Coal and gas **are two examples** of fossil fuels that cause greenhouse gases.

Exercise D. | Discussion   In this exercise, students can talk about their own country or any country that they know well.

TIP   You may want to try putting students into groups of three. Have one student in each group act as a secretary and take notes on the examples mentioned. Then compare notes with other groups in the class.

IDEAS FOR...   Expansion

Organize a team competition where each team is given a topic and has to come up with as many examples as they can within a minute. Topics can be general (music, sports, animals) or can include themes related to the topic of this unit (energy sources, ways to save energy, effects of global warming, etc.).

Grammar: The Simple Present and the Present Continuous

Read and go over the information in the box.

IDEAS FOR...   Presenting Grammar

Draw a time line on the board to illustrate the difference between something that is happening right now and something that you do regularly.

Exercise A.

- Have students complete the exercises individually. Then ask volunteers to read their answers aloud and explain the reasons for their choices.

Answer Key
2. is watching 3. receives
4. drink 5. takes

Exercise B.

- Have students complete the sentences individually. Then ask volunteers to read their answers aloud and explain the reasons for their choices.

Answer Key

2. Paul is studying right now. / Right now Paul is studying.
3. Isabel is taking four classes.
4. I turn off my computer at night.
5. Carmen and Luis speak three languages.
6. We are taking English classes. (= right now) / We take English classes. (= every semester)

Exercise C.

- Ask students to work in pairs to complete and practice the conversations.
- Encourage them to continue each conversation with their own ideas.

TIP Have students write their own conversations, leaving blanks for the verbs. Then they can exchange conversations with another pair and try to find the answers.

Answer Key *(Some answers may vary.)*

2. **A:** walk **B:** is raining / isn't nice out
3. **A:** do you do / are you doing **B:** I'm a scientist / I'm reading (Note: Both answers are possible, but **B**'s answer will vary according to the choice made in **A**.)
4. **A:** Does Marissa go **B:** is sick / is on vacation
5. **A:** Am I calling, Are you eating **B:** am watching TV.

 # Speaking *(page 31)*

30-45 mins

Discussing Personal Energy Use

Critical Thinking Focus: Interpreting Pie Charts

- Read the information in the box. Explain how pie charts can show information visually so that it is easier to understand.
- You may decide to contrast this pie chart with other types of graphs such as bar graphs.

Exercise A. | Understanding Visuals

- Discuss the questions and encourage students to ask further questions. For example: *Besides computers, what other appliances are found in houses? Why do you think so much energy is needed for heating and cooling?*

Exercise B. | Self-Reflection

- Allow time for students to think carefully about their answers and write them down.

Exercise C. | Critical Thinking

- If possible, students can create their pie charts on a computer.

Exercise D. | Discussion

- Students can work in pairs or groups to discuss these questions.
- Ask volunteers to summarize the main points of their discussions for the class.

TIP Display the pie charts on a wall or bulletin board. This will give students the chance to learn from each other's work.

IDEAS FOR... Checking Comprehension

Ask students to exchange pie charts with another student. They can use the information in their partner's pie chart to create a bar graph. (You can show students an example of a bar graph on page 216 of the *Independent Student Handbook*.) Students hand back their charts and check each other's work.

Viewing: Alternative Energy *(pages 32-33)*

30 mins

Overview of the Video | This video looks at the issue of whether alternative energy can be commercially competitive.

Before Viewing

Exercise A. | Prior Knowledge

- Ask students to look at the photos and read the captions.

- Explain the meaning of *alternative energy* (renewable energy, not from fossil fuels such as oil and coal).

- Have students identify each form of alternative energy in the pictures.

- With the class, discuss what one benefit or disadvantage of each form of energy could be.

Answer Key

From left to right: wind power, solar power, biomass, hydroelectric power

Exercise B. | Predicting Content Brainstorm possible vocabulary to describe forms of energy such as *clean, efficient, safe, expensive, dangerous,* and *cheap.*

TIP **As a way to prepare students for the video, you may want to play the first part of the video with the sound turned off and ask students to describe what they think is happening.**

While Viewing

Exercise A.
4:50
- Discuss which words from the previous exercise were mentioned in the video.

Exercise B.
4:50
- Discuss students' reactions to the photo of a wind farm. Is it beautiful? Why or why not?

- Allow time for students to read through the questions before watching.

- Play the video straight through and have students compare answers.

- Go over the answers as a class.

Answer Key   1. T 2. F 3. F 4. T 5. F 6. T

Exercise C.
4:50
- Allow time for students to read the sentences and see if they can complete any of them before watching the video again.

- Play the video a second time.

- Ask volunteers to read their answers aloud.

- Encourage students to ask you about the meaning of any new words such as viable, sustainable, efficient, and cost-effective.

Answer Key   1. agricultural 2. future 3. sells
4. alternative 5. countries

After Viewing

Critical Thinking

- Students could also work in groups to discuss their answers. A spokesperson from each group could summarize the discussion for the class.

- Question 4 will help prepare students for the next part of the unit. Make a list of their ideas on the board.

> **IDEAS FOR...   Expansion**
>
> Put students in groups and have them role-play the following situation:
>
> **Student A:** You want to put up a wind turbine on your property to generate power for your home.
> **Student B:** You are an environmentalist who believes in alternative energy. You support Student A in this project.
> **Student C:** You are Student A's neighbor. You think wind turbines are ugly. You don't want to see one from your property.
> **Student D:** You work for a coal-mining company and think it is important to keep jobs in the industry.

Building and Using Vocabulary *(pages 34-35)*

30 mins

WARM-UP

The Lesson B target vocabulary is presented in the context of ways to save energy.

- Ask students to suggest some ways to cut back on energy use. Discuss what can be done by individuals and also by institutions such as schools, hospitals, factories, and offices.

Building Vocabulary

track 1-17

Exercise A. | Meaning from Context

- Look at the photo. Ask students what they think is the connection between the title and the picture.

- Play the audio while students read.

- Check if any of their ideas from the previous lesson came up in the reading.

- Ask which of these suggestions students have already tried

Exercise B.

- Encourage students to use the context to work out the meanings of the new words.

Answer Key	1. j 2. f 3. c 4. i 5. a 6. g 7. d 8. h 9. e 10. b

> **IDEAS FOR...** Expansion
>
> Ask students to come up with new sentences to illustrate the meanings of these words.

Using Vocabulary

Exercise A.

- Look at the photo and discuss ways to save (or waste) energy in the kitchen.

- Set a time limit for reading the text and filling in the missing words.

> **IDEAS FOR...** Multi-level Classes
>
> To make this exercise more challenging, encourage students to try and remember the words from the previous exercise.

- Compare ideas on how difficult each idea would be to carry out and why.

Answer Key

1. waste	5. consume	9. practical
2. Cut back on	6. Replace	10. target
3. local	7. percent	
4. Keep track of	8. gradual	

Exercise B. | Discussion Set a time limit for students to compare answers in pairs.

Exercise C. | Critical Thinking

- Put pairs together to make groups of four. Students need to evaluate each tip and choose the three most energy-saving ones.

- Ask students to explain their reasons for their choices.

Exercise D. | Reporting to the Class

- Ask a spokesperson from each group to present their selections and their reasons.

> **TIP** While students are working, move around the classroom and note down any examples of students using the new vocabulary from the lesson. Review them at the end of the lesson.

> **IDEAS FOR...** Expansion
>
> Ask students to . . .
> - make a list of five additional ideas for saving energy.
> - make a poster persuading people to save energy.
> - make a questionnaire for a class survey to find out about how people save energy.

Developing Listening Skills
(pages 36-37)

45 mins

Pronunciation: Using Intonation to Show Feelings
track 1-18

- Read the information in the box and play the audio.

- Have students practice saying the two sentences with different intonation patterns.

Exercise A.
track 1-19

- Do the first sentence as an example.

- Students only need to identify the intonation pattern, not the feeling.

Answer Key	1. A: up B: down 2. A: up B: down 3. A: up B: up

Exercise B. | Play the audio again and check the answers as a class.
track 1-19

Answer Key	1. surprised, afraid 2. surprised, angry 3. happy, surprised

Exercise C.

- Ask volunteers to read the conversation aloud in two or three different ways.

- Allow time for students to work on their conversation in pairs.

Exercise D. | Presentation

- Each pair of students can present their conversation to the class while the other students guess their feelings.

Before Listening

Prior Knowledge | Discuss which appliances use the most electricity and whether these appliances are useful or necessary.

Answer Key	a. computer b. air conditioner c. hair dryer d. TV e. refrigerator f. clothes dryer

Listening: An Informal Conversation

Exercise A. | **Listening for Main Ideas**
track 1-20

- Play the first part of the audio and discuss the answers as a class.

Answer Key	1. the father of a family 2. upset 3. his electric bill is too high

Exercise B. | **Listening for Details**   Read the phrases in the box. Then play the second part of the audio.
track 1-21

Answer Key

Students should check the following ideas: replacing the light bulbs, using solar energy, eating cold food more often, keeping track of their energy use, taking shorter showers, turning the computers off at night, not using the hair dryer

Exercise C. | Play the audio again and have students check their answers.
track 1-21

Answer Key

replacing the light bulbs, turning the computers off at night

---

IDEAS FOR...   Checking Comprehension

Ask these additional questions orally or write them on the board.

1. What kind of light bulbs does Jason mention? (*energy-efficient light bulbs*)
2. Why doesn't Jason like Diana's hair dryer? (*It uses a lot of electricity, and it's noisy.*)
3. How much do they want to decrease their energy use by? (*by 10 percent next month*)
4. Why does Diana suggest eating sandwiches for lunch? (*because they wouldn't need to use the stove for cooking*)

After Listening

Critical Thinking | Encourage students to evaluate the information on the audio and relate it to the speakers' points of view.

30 mins

Exploring Spoken English
(pages 38-39)

Grammar: Modals of Advice—
*Should/Shouldn't, Ought to,
Had Better*

> **IDEAS FOR...**   **Presenting Grammar**
>
> Tell the class about a problem. For example: *I have too much housework, and I can't finish it.* Elicit advice. On the board, note the expressions students use to give you advice.

- Read the information in the box and point out important differences among the modals forms. (*Should* and *had better* are not followed by *to*. *Ought to* is not used in questions. *Had better* is often contracted to *'d better* or *'d better not*. It is not used in questions; use *should* instead.)

Exercise A.

- Allow time for students to choose the correct form of the modals to complete the sentences. Then check the answers as a class.

Answer Key	2. had better not 3. ought 4. shouldn't 5. had better

Exercise B.

- While students are practicing, monitor them to make notes of any errors.
- Have students switch roles as well as partners during this activity.

Language Function: Giving Advice and Making Suggestions

- Read the examples in the box.
- Ask students for suggestions about who might say these sentences and in what situations.

Exercise A. | Self-Reflection

- Give some examples of different problems (true or fictional).
- Ask for possible solutions and elicit advice that uses expressions from the box.
- Give students time to write their own problems.

Exercise B.

- Have students work in pairs to practice the conversations.
- Walk around the classroom to monitor their use of the expressions for giving advice and making suggestions.
- Invite volunteers to perform their conversations for the class.

> **IDEAS FOR...**   **Multi-level Classes**
>
> Have students of similar levels work together. Lower-level students can go slowly enough to ensure comprehension, and higher-level students can challenge each other by using more difficult dialog.

Exercise C. | Role-Playing

- Ask for some suggestions for how to start off this conversation. Students can then continue in pairs.
- Have students write the conversation for homework.

> **TIP**   While students are practicing, monitor them to make sure they are using a variety of modals of advice and expressions for making suggestions.

> **IDEAS FOR...**   **Expansion**
>
> Ask each student to write down one difficulty with reducing energy use. For example: *I want to drive my car less often, but there are no buses in my area.* Then have them role-play asking for and giving advice. When they have finished, they can pass their problem on to another pair and switch roles.

Engage: Planning a Group Presentation *(page 40)*

45 mins

WARM-UP

- Discuss different strategies for saving energy in your school.

- Ask questions such as the following: *Does your school recycle? What do they recycle? Do they use energy-efficient light bulbs? If not, why not?*

Exercise A.

- Read the information or ask a volunteer to read it aloud.

- Ask some comprehension check questions. *What is the Green Committee? Why are they going to meet? What do they have to do?*

Exercise B. | Brainstorming

- Remind students that the purpose of brainstorming is to generate as many ideas as possible. They should write them down on a large piece of paper scattered around the page in any order. Later they will evaluate them and choose the best ideas.

Student to Student: Taking Turns

- Explain that taking turns encourages group cooperation. Working well on a team is an essential skill in most work and academic settings.

Exercise C.

- In this stage of the planning process, students will evaluate their ideas. Encourage them to identify their criteria for evaluating them. Their criteria may include practicality and cost-effectiveness of the energy-saving ideas.

> **TIP** You may decide to appoint one person in each group as a leader to make sure everyone has a turn.

Presentation Skills: Organizing Ideas for a Group Presentation

- Read the information in the box.

- Remind students to use these skills when doing exercise **D**.

Exercise D. | Planning a Presentation

- Remind students that they will have to provide an introduction and a conclusion for their presentation.

- Each person should be clear about what information he or she is going to present.

- Students should practice in groups first.

Exercise E. | Presentation

- Before students begin their presentations, you may want to clarify with your class some of the criteria for evaluating a good presentation. The criteria could include clear organization, eye contact with audience, as well as good visuals and diagrams.

- Students can use the criteria to evaluate each other's presentations.

> **TIP** You may decide to videotape these presentations for later discussion.

IDEAS FOR... Expansion

In class or for homework, students can write a letter to the staff and students of the school giving them some suggestions and advice for reducing energy consumption in the school and persuading them to take action.

Culture and Tradition

Academic Track
Anthropology/Sociology

Academic Pathways:

Lesson A: Listening to a Lecture
Giving Information

Lesson B: Listening to an Assignment
and a Student Presentation
Planning a Presentation

Unit Theme

In many countries, traditional ways of life are being forgotten as more people move away from their homes in rural areas and move to cities. Some people see this as a sign that their lives are improving while others regret losing traditional beliefs and customs.

Unit 3 explores the topic of culture and tradition as it relates to:
– cowboy life and culture in the United States and Mexico
– gauchos in Argentina
– Roma music in Europe
– traditional musical instruments

Think and Discuss *(page 41)*

5 mins

- Ask students to describe the photo and read the caption. What are the riders doing? (*herding horses*)

- Find out what students know about cowboys and make a list on the board. What were cowboys' lives like in the past and what are they like nowadays? What was good or difficult about their lives in the past? Nowadays?

- Mexico has a long cowboy tradition that predates that of other regions in North America. Other places that have cowboy traditions include Hawaii (*paniolos*), Australia (*stockmen*), Argentina, Uruguay, Paraguay, and southern Brazil (*gauchos*), Peru and Chile (*huasos*), and Venezuela (*llaneros*).

Exploring the Theme: Culture and Tradition *(pages 42-43)*

15 mins

The opening spread features a world map and pictures of people in traditional clothes.

- Ask students to describe each photo and match them with the correct location on the map.

- Ask: *What are the people wearing? What do you think their lifestyle is like?*

- Discuss questions 1–4. Ask: *Is it important for these people to keep their traditions? Does it matter if traditions are lost?*

- Ask if students know of other people who are trying to preserve their traditional culture.

- Ask which one of these cultures students would like to learn more about. You may decide to give a research project on the culture as an out-of-class assignment.

IDEAS FOR...   **Checking Comprehension**

Ask additional questions about the texts on this page.
1. Which descriptions mention dance as part of their tradition? (*Geisha and Navajo*)
2. Which descriptions mention language as part of their tradition? (*Roma, Navajo, and Aborigine*)
3. Which group of people lives in the mountains? (*Sherpa*)
4. Which group of people speaks many different languages? (*Aborigine*)
5. Why do Roma children stop speaking the language? (*because they do not use their language in school*)

Pronunciation Note
Navajo: **nav**-uh-hoe

Building and Using Vocabulary *(pages 44-45)*

30 mins

WARM-UP

The Lesson A target vocabulary is presented in the context of cowboy life and culture.

- Ask students to suggest some advantages and disadvantages of this lifestyle.
- Discuss some reasons why this lifestyle may be disappearing.

Building Vocabulary

Critical Thinking Focus: Inferring Meaning from Context

- Discuss why it is important to be able to infer meaning from context. (*Because the meaning of a word changes according to the context, you have to be able to choose from a range of definitions given in a dictionary.*)

Exercise A. | Meaning from Context

track 1-22

- Do the first item as an example. Show how the second sentence gives you more information about the meaning of the word highlighted in blue.
- Encourage students to do the exercise without referring to their dictionaries.
- Play the audio and allow time for students to check their answers.

Answer Key

1. haven't	**5.** No one	**9.** don't know
2. long	**6.** areas	**10.** cause of
3. making plans for	**7.** keep	
4. usually	**8.** all die	

Exercise B.

- Remind students to use the context to work out the meanings of these words.

Answer Key	**1.** c **2.** j **3.** h **4.** a **5.** i **6.** b **7.** d **8.** f **9.** g **10.** e

Using Vocabulary

Exercise A.

- Look at the photo and ask students to describe what is happening.
- Have students read the article and try to guess the words without looking back at page 44.
- Then have them check their answers using exercise **B** on page 44.
- Point out that they may have to change the form of the word (see items 4 and 7).

Answer Key

1. region	**5.** customs	**9.** preserve
2. factor	**6.** traditional	**10.** still
3. estimate	**7.** disappeared	
4. developed	**8.** endangered	

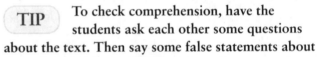

TIP To check comprehension, have the students ask each other some questions about the text. Then say some false statements about the article and have students correct you.

Exercise B. | Self-Reflection

- Allow time for students to complete the sentences individually.
- Put students into small groups to compare their answers and get more information from each other.
- Discuss the answers as a class.

Pronunciation Note
Inuit: **in**-oo-it

Developing Listening Skills
(pages 46-47)

track 1-23

Pronunciation: Reduced Function Words

- Read the information in the box. Explain and demonstrate the meaning of *reduced forms*. They are words that are not stressed and are run together in speaking. Contractions are a way of writing some reduced forms, but others are not usually shown in writing.

- Play the audio and ask students to repeat the sentences. Ask students which words are reduced in the examples.

Exercise A. | Encourage students to read the passage quietly and circle the words they think may be reduced.

track 1-24 **Exercise B. |** Play the audio, pausing and replaying so that students can check their answers.

Exercise C. | Have students work in pairs and help each other with pronunciation.

Before Listening

Exercise A. | Using a Dictionary After completing this exercise, ask students to make up some sentences using these words to describe the photo or cowboys in general.

Answer Key 1. f 2. c 3. e 4. b 5. d 6. a

Exercise B. | Prior Knowledge Discuss the questions as a class. Make a list of questions students still have about cowboys.

Listening: A Lecture

track 1-25 **Exercise A. | Listening for Main Ideas**

- Play the audio while students listen for the main ideas.

Answer Key 1. Wyoming, USA 2. Coahuila, Mexico

track 1-25 **Exercise B. | Listening for Details**

- Read the notes and discuss what kind of information is missing. Play the audio again while students complete the notes.

- Have students compare answers with each other before playing the audio again.

Answer Key

Tyrel	2 years old older brother 2300 electricity enjoyed
Manuel	4 years old 4 married move

track 1-25 **Exercise C. | Making Inferences** When going over the answers, make sure students explain what evidence in the lecture they based their answer choices on.

Answer Key 1. F 2. F 3. T 4. F

IDEAS FOR... **Checking Comprehension**

Ask these additional questions or write them on the board.
1. Why did Robb Kendrick travel around America? (*to record cowboys' way of life in a book*)
2. What time of year did Tyrel and his brother take care of cattle? (*December to April*)
3. When did the cowboy tradition start in Mexico? (*in the 1600s*)

After Listening

Critical Thinking | Encourage students to make generalizations based on the information in the lecture. They may come up with a list of typical characteristics that represent a cowboy's way of life.

Exploring Spoken English

45 mins

(pages 48-50)

Language Function: Asking for and Giving Clarification

■ Read the information in the box. Ask for some suggestions for phrases you could use to ask for clarification.

 Exercise A.
track 1-26

■ Play the audio while students read the conversation.

■ Have students work in groups of three to practice reading the conversation aloud.

> **IDEAS FOR... Multi-level Classes**
>
> Higher-level students can practice the conversation without looking at the text. Lower-level students can read the text as they practice it. Invite students to choose the level of challenge they want.

Exercise B.

■ Write the chart on the board and invite students to tell you what phrases to write in each column.

■ Ask for further ideas to add to each column. Add: *What does . . . mean? What is meant by . . . ?*

Answer Key

Asking for clarification	Giving clarification
• Are there still cowboys today?	• Let me explain.
• Could you explain that?	• What I mean is . . .
• I still don't understand.	
• So, what you mean is that . . .	
• Do you mean that . . . ?	

Exercise C.

■ Allow time for students to complete the sentences with their own ideas.

■ Put students in pairs to practice asking for and giving clarification.

■ Call on several pairs to say one of their short conversations for the class.

> **IDEAS FOR... Expansion**
>
> Ask students to choose a topic related to the theme of this unit. Invite three or four volunteers to form a panel of experts on this topic. Ask them to sit at the front of the class. They will give a talk about one aspect of the topic while members of the "audience" interrupt them to ask for clarification.

Grammar: The Past Continuous Tense

Read the information in the box.

> **IDEAS FOR... Presenting Grammar**
>
> Ask students to ask and answer questions about what they were doing at specific moments of time in the past.
> For example:
> S1: What were you doing at 6 P.M. yesterday afternoon?
> S2: I was doing my homework.

Exercise A. | Ask: *Which sentence describes an activity that was going on before a specific point in the past? (3) Which sentence describes two actions happening at the same time? (2) Which sentence describes a past activity that was going on at a particular time? (1)*

Answer Key

Students should circle the following verbs:

1. was working

2. was working, were playing

3. was riding

Pronunciation Note
charro: **chahr**-oh
charreadas: chair-ee-**ah**-duhs
vaqueros: vah-**kair**-ohs

Exercise B.

- Allow time for students to complete the sentences.

- Note that two answers (9 and 10) need to be in the present continuous. See if students can tell you which answers require this tense.

- Ask volunteers to read their answers aloud for the class.

Answer Key

2. was living 3. was cleaning, was watching

4. wasn't raining 5. was waiting 6. were sleeping

7. was eating, was talking 8. was riding 9. is exercising

10. are . . . drinking

Exercise C.

- Ask students to work in pairs to practice questions and answers using the past continuous.

- Encourage them to continue each conversation with their own ideas.

Speaking *(page 51)*

0-45 mins

Giving Information

Exercise A.

- Put students into groups of three.

- Assign each person in the group a different text to read.

- Set a time limit for reading the texts.

> **TIP** If you do not have equal groups of three in your class, you can ask two students to share one text in a group of four.

Exercise B. | Note-Taking

- Explain that each student should tell the other two about what they have just read. The other two students close their books and take notes, asking for clarification if necessary.

- Encourage students to ask you questions about the vocabulary in these texts.

> **IDEAS FOR... Expansion**
>
> Ask students to make new groups and retell the information they heard from their previous group using their notes. The other students can correct them by looking at the book or asking for clarification.

> **IDEAS FOR... Checking Comprehension**
>
> Ask students to read all three texts and use the information to complete a chart listing what these three types of cowboys have in common and what is different about them. You may want to use a Venn diagram like the one on page 214 of the *Independent Student Handbook* with three overlapping circles.

Exercise C. | Critical Thinking

- Have students work in groups of three.

- Suggest that students record their ideas in a chart or other graphic organizer.

> **IDEAS FOR... Multi-level Classes**
>
> To make this task more challenging, have students read their texts from exercise **B** and take notes. Then they can tell the other students about their text using their notes. Afterwards they can check to see if all the points were included.

Pronunciation Note
paniolo: pah-nee-**oh**-loh

Viewing: The Gauchos of Argentina *(pages 52-53)*

30-45 mins

Overview of the Video | This video looks at the lifestyle of gauchos in Argentina. Note that this video is 9 minutes and 26 seconds long. You may need to consider how much class time is remaining when you start the video.

Before Viewing

Exercise A. | Using a Dictionary

- Ask students to look at the photos and read the captions.
- Check the answers to the exercise as a class.

Answer Key   1. c 2. e 3. d 4. a 5. b

Exercise B. | Prior Knowledge

- Remind students of the text about *gauchos* (Student 3) on the previous page.
- Call on students to read their answers aloud.

Answer Key

1. South America 2. remote places 3. different from 4. an old and proud tradition 5. Animals

While Viewing

Exercise A.
9:26
- Play the video and check the answers to the previous exercise.

Exercise B.
9:26
- Allow time for students to read the sentences before watching the video.
- Play the video and go over the answers as a class.

Answer Key   1. F 2. T 3. F 4. T 5. T 6. T

Exercise C.
9:26
- Ask students to try to remember the information. Point out that all the answers are numbers.
- Play the video (or part of the video) again.

Answer Key   1. three 2. 76 3. 154 4. 150,000 5. 19th 6. 1800

After Viewing

Critical Thinking

- Students can work in groups to discuss their answers.
- Ask a spokesperson from each group to summarize the discussion for the class.
- Question 4 helps prepare students for the next part of the unit.

TIP   While students are presenting their ideas, encourage other students to ask for clarification.

> **IDEAS FOR...   Expansion**
> Ask students to work in pairs to role play an interview with a gaucho. Pairs can present their interview to the class.

Pronunciation Note
rhea: **ree**-uh

Building and Using Vocabulary *(pages 54-55)*

30 mins

WARM-UP

The Lesson B target vocabulary is presented in the context of different types of traditional music and musical instruments.

- Play some examples of different types of music and ask students to identify the instruments.

- Discuss why music is important to culture and what can be expressed through music.

Building Vocabulary

track 1-27

Exercise A. | Meaning from Context

- Ask students about their favorite kinds of music. Ask if they are interested in music from other countries.

- Explain that they will read some instructions for an oral presentation about music.

- Play the audio while students read.

Exercise B.

- Encourage students to use the context to work out the meanings.

- Point out that the words are all nouns or verbs and this can be a clue to matching them with their definitions.

- Ask students to come up with new sentences to illustrate the meanings of these words.

| **Answer Key** | **1. e 2. j 3. g 4. i 5. d 6. b 7. c** |
| | **8. f 9. a 10. h** |

> **IDEAS FOR...**   **Checking Comprehension**
>
> Write the following words on the board and ask students to use them to summarize the assignment: *select, describe, explain, compare, define, summarize*

Using Vocabulary

Exercise A.

- Set a time limit for reading the sentences and filling in the missing words.

- To make this exercise more challenging, encourage students to try to remember the words from the previous exercise without looking back.

- Remind students that some items may require a slightly different form of the word (item 4).

Answer Key		
1. select	5. contrast	9. rhythm
2. describe	6. define	10. lyrics
3. explain	7. summarize	
4. compare	8. instrument	

Exercise B. | Discussion   Have students work in groups. Each student should take turns speaking for 30 seconds.

> **TIP**   To encourage students to evaluate each other, give them a set of criteria they can use to give each other a score. The criteria could include fluency, creativity, good vocabulary, etc.

> **IDEAS FOR...**   **Multi-level Classes**
>
> For an additional challenge, ask a few volunteers to bring in an audio clip of their favorite song or music track. They can give a short talk about the musician, what the song means to them, and why they like it.

Developing Listening Skills

45 mins

(pages 56-57)

Before Listening

- Look at the photo and the map.

- Read the text and encourage students to ask questions about it.

- Read the questions and find out what students already know about the Roma.

- Make a list of students' additional questions on the board. They might include the following: *Why did the Roma move from India to Europe? What kinds of musical instruments do they play?* (Some of these questions can be followed up for homework.)

- If possible, bring in an example of Roma music.

Listening: An Assignment and a Student Presentation

track 1-28 **Exercise A. | Note-Taking**

- Tell students that they will hear a professor explaining an assignment.

- Remind students it is important to understand the professor's instructions and take clear notes.

- Allow time for students to read the notes and think about what information is missing.

- Play the audio while students write their answers.

- Write the answers on the board.

Answer Key

1. select, music 2. culture 3. describe, explain, traditional, modern 4. contrast, music 5. play
6. main, questions

track 1-29 **Exercise B. | Listening for Main Ideas**

- Play the audio while students note the main ideas.

Answer Key

Students should circle:

1, 2, 3, 6

The student did not compare or contrast Roma music with another kind of music. (4)

The student did not play a sample of the music. (5)

Exercise C. | Listening for Details

- Allow time for students to read the sentences.

- Play the audio again while students circle the answers.

- Go over the answers as a whole group.

- Ask students to evaluate the presentation. What did they like about it? What do they think could be improved?

Answer Key

1. Europe 2. music 3. fast
4. strong 5. electronic 6. popular

IDEAS FOR... Checking Comprehension

Ask these additional questions or write them on the board.
1. What does the word *shukar* mean? (*fine or very good*)
2. What languages do the Roma speak? (*Romany and the language of the country they live in*)
3. What are the traditional Roma instruments? (*drums and cimbalom, which is a sort of piano*)

After Listening

Critical Thinking | Encourage students to compare and contrast music traditions in their country with those of the Roma.

Exploring Spoken English

(pages 58-59)

Language Function: Interrupting Politely

- Read the information in the box and ask students to practice saying the expressions.

- You may want to discuss how polite it is to interrupt a lecture or a conversation and when they would do so in their culture. In some cultures, for example, it shows active engagement with the speaker, but in others it might show lack of respect.

Exercise A.

- Look at the two photos and ask students to describe them.

- Have students work in pairs. Each person chooses one of the texts to read aloud. The other student interrupts with questions.

- Walk around the classroom while students are practicing to make sure they are using a range of interrupting expressions.

Exercise B. | Discussion

- Have students switch partners and discuss these questions, interrupting each other politely as they do so.

Grammar: Adjectives Ending in *-ed* and *-ing*

- Read the information in the box.

- Make a list of adjectives ending in *-ed* and *-ing* on the board. You may want to categorize them as positive or negative. For example, positive adjectives may include *fascinating*, *thrilling*, and *entertaining*; negative adjectives may include *frightening*, *tiring*, and *depressing*.

Exercise A.

- Allow time for students to complete the answers individually.

- Check the answers as a class.

> **IDEAS FOR... Multi-level Classes**
>
> To make this exercise more challenging, write the adjective pairs on the board, out of order. Then read the sentences aloud, leaving the adjectives out. Have students guess the missing word. More than one adjective may be correct. Encourage students to defend their answers.

Exercise B. | Role-Playing

- Have students work in pairs.

- Walk around the classroom to monitor language use.

- Invite volunteers to perform their conversations for the class.

- Give feedback on their use of adjectives with *-ed* and *-ing* endings.

> **IDEAS FOR... Expansion**
>
> Ask each student to write down one type of music they are very interested in and one type that they find boring on a small piece of paper. Collect the papers and redistribute them. Then have students walk around asking questions to find out whose paper they have. They can only use *yes/no* questions with *-ed* and *-ing* adjectives.
> For example:
> *Do you find rap music boring or exciting?*
> *Are you interested in opera or are you bored by it?*

TIP   Remind students to bring in a sample of their favorite music to use in the assignment on the next page.

Student to Student: Talking about Assignments | Tell students briefly about the presentation they will do on the next page. Then ask students to discuss it with their partner using the expressions in the box.

Engage: Planning a Presentation *(page 60)*

45 mins

WARM-UP

- Play short examples of different types of music (e.g., jazz, reggae, opera) and ask students to identify what types of music they are.

- Talk about your favorite kind of music and say why you like it and where it is from.

Exercise A. | Brainstorming

- This exercise can be done in groups or as a class.

- Invite students to come up to the board and have each one write the name of a different kind of music.

Exercise B.

- Tell each group to choose a type of music they like from the list they created in exercise **A**. You could ask them to make a first, second, and third choice to ensure that every group has a different topic.

> **TIP** It will be more interesting for the class if each group chooses a different type of music for their presentation. You can facilitate this by writing the names of the types of music on pieces of paper and putting them in a hat. A leader from each group will pick one paper randomly out of the hat. Another idea is to assign two or three types of music to each group and have each group vote on their choice.

Exercise C. | Collaboration

- Remind students to decide which part of the presentation each member will present. They should make sure everyone has an equal part. They should make notes about their parts, helping each other with ideas, and practice giving their presentation to their group.

> **TIP** You may decide to appoint one person in each group as a leader to make sure everyone participates.

Presentation Skills: Posture | Read the information in the box. Explain that positive body language helps to convey confidence and makes a presentation clearer. For example, if you stand up straight and look directly at your audience (not at your notes or at the board), your voice will be clearer and easier to follow. Demonstrate some examples of good and bad posture for giving presentations.

Exercise D. | Presentation

- Before students start their presentations, you may want to clarify the criteria for evaluating a presentation. These criteria could include clear organization, eye contact with audience, and good posture.

- Students can use the criteria to evaluate each other's presentations.

- Encourage students to ask questions for clarification during the talk.

> **TIP** You may decide to videotape these presentations for later discussion.

> **IDEAS FOR...** **Expansion**
>
> In class or for homework, students can write an essay on the topic of their presentation. The essays can then be posted to a class Web site or shared with a partner.

A Thirsty World

Academic Track
Interdisciplinary

Academic Pathways:
Lesson A: Listening to a Guest Speaker
Presenting an Idea
Lesson B: Listening to a Group Discussion
Role-Playing a Meeting

Unit Theme

This unit explores a topic that is essential for our lives—water. In many countries, there are extremes of drought or flooding, and managing water is a huge problem. In addition, global warming and climate change are having a big impact on countries with little water.

Unit 4 explores the topic of water as it relates to:
– storing and managing water
– providing clean water

– allocating water resources

Think and Discuss *(page 61)*

5 mins

- Ask students to describe the photo. Discuss who these people might be and what problems they may have with water.

- Ask students why some places do not have enough water. You may want to mention issues such as droughts, lack of rainfall, global warming, soil erosion, lack of water pipes, poor irrigation, and inadequate water facilities.

- Ask students what happens when there is too much water. You may want to discuss which countries are prone to floods, monsoons, and landslides.

- A second photo shows children using a PlayPump to collect water. There is more information about PlayPumps on page 70 of this unit.

- Discuss questions 1–3 with the class.

- Useful vocabulary includes *dam, reservoir, irrigation, hydroelectric power,* and *generate.*

> **IDEAS FOR...**   **Expansion**
>
> Ask students to work in groups to make a list of questions about other famous dams or things they would like to know about the construction of dams. For homework, ask them to research the answers to these questions and be prepared to tell the class what they found out.

Exploring the Theme:
A Thirsty World *(pages 62-63)*

15 mins

The opening spread features a photo of a river in Iceland.

- Ask students if they have ever visited a dam or a reservoir. Invite them to tell the class about their visit.

- A smaller photo shows the Hoover Dam in the United States, built in the 1930s. Ask students to describe the photo and locate this dam on a map of the United States.

Building and Using Vocabulary *(pages 64-65)*

30 mins

WARM-UP

The Lesson A target vocabulary is presented in the context of a quiz about water facts.

- Ask students what they know about water.

- Brainstorm a list of general knowledge questions about water. For example: *How is rain formed? Where is the largest lake in the world?* See how many questions students can answer.

Building Vocabulary

track 1-30

Exercise A. | Meaning from Context

- Explain that students should listen, read the sentences, and try to understand the words in blue. Explain that some sentences are true and some are false.

- Play the audio.

- Allow time for students to discuss the words in blue in pairs. They can translate them or try to think of synonyms in English.

Exercise B. | Remind students to use the context to work out the meaning of these words. Discuss any differences between the definitions they come up with and those in their dictionaries.

Answer Key	1. f 2. j 3. c 4. h 5. d 6. b 7. g 8. e 9. a 10. i

Exercise C. | Ask students to look back at the quiz in exercise **A** and choose **T** for *true* or **F** for *false* for each sentence. They can check their answers and see correct information for the false statements on page 65 of the Student Book.

- Which answers did many students get wrong?

- Which statements were the most surprising and why?

Using Vocabulary

Exercise A.

- Look at the photo and ask students what they know about the Amazon River. *The Amazon River is 3202 miles (6280 kilometers) long. Its source is in the Andes Mountains in Peru. The mouth or delta is in northeastern Brazil. It is the world's second longest river. (The Nile in Africa is the longest.)*

- Have students read the sentences and try to guess the words without looking back on page 64.

- Have students check their answers using exercise **B** on the previous page.

Answer Key		
1. flows	5. clean	9. enough
2. require	6. provide	10. available
3. resource	7. amount	
4. collect	8. manage	

> **TIP** Ask students to choose four of the vocabulary words and make up some additional sentences using them. They can record their sentences in their vocabulary notebooks.

Exercise B. | Discussion

- Put students into pairs.

- Allow time for students to discuss their answers.

- Ask a spokesperson for each pair to report to the class.

- Encourage students to use vocabulary introduced in this lesson.

Developing Listening Skills
(pages 66-67)

Before Listening

Using a Dictionary

- Ask students to use their dictionaries to check the meanings of these words. Ask them if there are other forms of these words (verbs, adjectives, etc.).

Listening: A Guest Speaker

Exercise A. | Listening for Main Ideas

track 1-31

- Explain the meaning of *gorge* (a deep, narrow valley with steep sides) and ask students to describe what they think the Three Gorges Dam is like.

- Read the sentences aloud.

- Play the audio.

- Take a class vote on what the main idea is.

- Discuss why they think this is the main idea. (One clue is in the conclusion: Although the Three Gorges Dam was extremely expensive to build and caused some problems in the region, its benefits are much more significant. The other three statements are mentioned in the lecture, but as details, not the main idea.)

Answer Key	There are both benefits and risks to the Three Gorges Dam.

Exercise B. | Listening for Details

track 1-31

- Allow time for students to read the notes.

- Play the audio again while students complete the notes.

Answer Key

- Size: **1.4** miles long, **607** feet tall • Reservoir: **410** miles long • more than **126,000** workers • **renewable source** of energy • **300,000** people were killed • **larger ships** can travel • **land** underwater • **towns** and villages • **one million** people • **old** historical and cultural sites • impact on the **environment** • **largest** dams • important **benefits** • significant **risks**

IDEAS FOR... Checking Comprehension

Ask additional questions about the listening or write them on the board.

1. What kind of energy is produced by the dam? (*hydroelectricity*)
2. What percentage of China's energy is produced by the dam? (*three percent*)
3. Where is the energy used? (*in people's homes and on farms*)
4. Why is it clean? (*It doesn't produce greenhouse gases.*)

After Listening

Critical Thinking

- Have students work in pairs.

- Encourage them to think about the information in the talk from different points of view.

- Discuss their answers and the reasons as a whole class.

Pronunciation: Syllable Stress

track 1-32

- Read the information in the box.

- Review the meaning of the word *syllable.*

- Ask students to count the syllables in the three words and identify the stressed one in each word.

Exercise A.

track 1-33

- Play the audio and go over the answers as a class.

Answer Key

1. a(vai)la ble 2. sig(ni)fi cant 3. in for(ma)tion
4. un der(stand) 5. vo(ca)bu la ry 6. pro nun ci (a)tion
7. (di)ffi cult 8. im(por)tant 9. (ne)ces sa ry 10. con ser(va)tion

Exercise B.

track 1-34

Answer Key

1. (val)u able (re)source 2. (ma)naged, (dan)ger ous
3. e (con)omy 4. (prob)a bly dis ap(pear)

Pronunciation Note

Yangtze: yang-see

45 mins

Exploring Spoken English
(pages 68-70)

Language Function: Talking about Priorities

- Read the information in the box.

- Have students practice saying the sentences with correct stress and intonation.

Exercise A.

- Read the sentences aloud.

- Have students come up with their own sentences using the expressions they underlined.

Answer Key

1. is a priority
2. The main thing is
3. The most important

Exercise B.

- Allow time for students to complete the chart individually.

- Invite volunteers to tell the class one of their priorities and their reasons for it.

Exercise C. | Discussion

- Put students into pairs to compare answers.

- Encourage them to give reasons for their opinions and agree and disagree politely.

Exercise D. | Self-Reflection

- Students can work in pairs to discuss and write their ideas.

Exercise E.

- Have each pair join up with another pair to compare and discuss their ideas.

- You may want to make these topics less abstract by rephrasing them. For example: *What is one thing you want to improve in our school or our city?*

> **IDEAS FOR...**   **Multi-level Classes**
>
> Allow enough time for students to cover two topics. Those students who finish more quickly can do more.

Grammar: The Passive Voice

Read the information in the box. If appropriate, point out that the passive voice is formed by using the verb *be* (present or past) and the past participle of the verb. Call out some regular and irregular verbs and ask students to tell you the past participle.

Exercise A.

- Allow time for students to complete the sentences individually.

- Remind students to use *by* plus the agent.

- Invite volunteers to write their answers on the board.

Answer Key

2. This was made by my sister.
3. Chinese is spoken by over 1 billion people.
4. Isabel was asked by the teacher to give a presentation.
5. This delicious cake was baked by Oscar.
6. That restaurant is owned by a friendly man.

Student to Student: Showing Surprise | Read the information in the box and have students practice the expressions using the appropriate intonation.

Exercise B. | Discussion

- Put students into pairs to ask and answer questions using the passive.

- Encourage students to extend their conversations and use expressions for showing surprise.

Exercise C. | Understanding Visuals

- Explain that diagrams are a useful way of conveying information about a process. The arrows and the numbers in this diagram help the reader to understand how a PlayPump works.

- Ask students to look at the diagram and describe what they think is happening.

- Read the text aloud.

Exercise D.

- Ask students to complete this exercise orally and then write their answers in their notebooks.

- Ask students to cover the sentences they wrote and have them explain the process in pairs one more time while looking at the diagram and using the passive voice.

Answer Key

1. The merry-go-round is turned by the children.
2. The energy is used to pump water.
3. 369 gallons (1400 liters) of clean water are pumped in one hour.
4. The water is stored in a big tank.
5. The water is carried to people's houses.
6. Water is pumped up to the tank.
7. Ads are painted on the sides of the tank.

Speaking *(page 71)*

0-45 mins

Presenting an Idea

Exercise A.

- Put students into groups of three.

- Read the situation and explain that each group will choose one device to present.

- Allow time for students to read the texts and choose a device.

Exercise B. | Planning a Presentation

- Explain that each group will present their chosen device to the class, and each member of the group will give one part of the presentation.

TIP Monitor students as they are working and note any problems with their usage of the passive voice. You can use your notes when giving feedback later.

Exercise C. | Presentation

- Invite each group to take turns presenting their device to the class.

- Tell the class to vote on the best presentation.

- Encourage the class to ask further questions about information that is not presented here, such as the cost of the Water Cone and the KickStart Pump, or the amount of water moved/pumped by the KickStart Pump.

Viewing: More Water for India (pages 72-73)

30 mins

Overview of the Video | This video looks at the problems of insufficient water in India. It describes a successful new project to build small dams in rural areas.

Before Viewing

Exercise A. | Using a Dictionary

- Ask students to look at the photos and read the captions.

- Compare and contrast the two photos.

- Ask students to use their dictionaries to match the words and their definitions.

- Ask students to use the words to make sentences about the photos.

Answer Key   1. c 2. b 3. e 4. a 5. d

Critical Thinking Focus: Predicting Content

- Read the information in the box aloud. Explain how predicting helps readers integrate new information (what they are going to read) with information they already know.

Exercise B. | Predicting Content

- Tell students to look at the photos and the video title. Ask them to brainstorm ideas for what the video could be about.

- Have students make a list of words they might expect to hear in the video.

While Viewing

Exercise A.
4:08

- Play the video and ask students to circle any words from the previous exercise that they hear.

Exercise B.
4:08

- Allow time for students to read the sentences before watching the video.

- Play the video.

- Go over the answers as a class.

Answer Key

1. New Delhi 2. New Delhi and Alwar 3. New Delhi
4. Alwar 5. Alwar 6. New Delhi 7. New Delhi

Exercise C.
4:08

- Allow time for students to read the sentences before watching the video again.

- Go over the answers as a class.

Answer Key   1. river 2. gallons 3. dams
4. small 5. green 6. 800

After Viewing

Exercise A.

- Ask students to rewrite the sentences in the passive voice and then read them aloud.

- Invite volunteers to write their answers on the board.

Answer Key

2. A lot of water is required by the people in New Delhi.

3. Water is delivered to people by trucks.

4. An organization to help people was started by Rajendra Singh.

Exercise B. | Critical Thinking

- For question 1, direct each student in the group to list one advantage and one disadvantage. For questions 1 and 2, students can pool their ideas in a group before sharing them with the class. If there is time, invite two volunteers to come to the board and make a list of ideas from the class discussion.

- Question 2 will help prepare students for the next part of the unit. Make a list of students' ideas on the board.

IDEAS FOR...   Checking Comprehension

Ask students to compare and contrast the large dam in China and the small ones in India. What is similar and what is different about the reasons for building them and their benefits? What problems do they share?

Building and Using Vocabulary *(pages 74-75)*

WARM-UP

The Lesson B target vocabulary is presented in the context of how to conserve water.

- Brainstorm words connected to water and write them on the board.

- Brainstorm ways to describe water and how it affects our lives.

Building Vocabulary

Exercise A. | Meaning from Context

- Look at the photo and the title of the text and ask students to predict the content.

- Play the audio while students read.

- Ask students to suggest alternative words for the words in blue.

> **IDEAS FOR...** Checking Comprehension
>
> To check comprehension, ask students to summarize the main ideas of the text in two or three sentences.

Exercise B. | Discussion

- Encourage students to relate the information in the text to their own lives.

Exercise C.

- To make this exercise more challenging, encourage students to try to complete the sentences without looking at the words in the box. Tell them to look back at the text in exercise **A** for context clues.

Answer Key

1. allocate	5. urgent	9. Extremely
2. Industry	6. crisis	10. scarce
3. normal	7. Domestic	
4. Agriculture	8. experience	

Using Vocabulary

Exercise A. | Self-Reflection

- Allow time for students to reflect on the statements and complete the survey.

- Answer any questions about vocabulary.

Exercise B. | Discussion

- Have students work in groups to compare and explain their answers.

- Remind them to give reasons for their opinions and to use language for talking about priorities (page 68).

> **TIP** To ensure that the discussions flow smoothly, you may want to assign roles to each person in the group. One person can be a facilitator, making sure that everyone speaks. Another can be a note-taker, summarizing the different opinions.

Exercise C. | Presentation

- Have each group choose a spokesperson to present a summary of the group's discussion to the class.

> **IDEAS FOR...** Expansion
>
> Ask students to make a list of ways that people waste water in their country and make some suggestions for how to conserve it.

Developing Listening Skills

45 mins

(pages 76-77)

Before Listening

Exercise A. | Understanding Visuals

■ Ask questions about the two maps. What part of Australia is this region in? What period of time does the map refer to? What do the different shades of brown mean on the map?

Answer Key *(Answers may vary.)*

1. It was mainly below or much below average.
2. There was less rain than usual in this period of time.
3. They probably have drought conditions and problems with lack of water.

Exercise B. | Ask students to report any misunderstandings or differences of opinion and discuss them with the class.

Listening: A Group Discussion

 Exercise A. | Listening for Main Ideas

track 1-36

■ Play the audio while students number the pictures.

Answer Key

2	3
4	1

Exercise B. | Listening for Details

track 1-36

■ Allow time for students to read the sentences.

■ Play the audio again.

Answer Key

1. seven 2. 500, 70, grass 3. farmers 4. vacation, hotels 5. a million, 21,000 6. cities 7. gardens

 Exercise C. | Note-Taking Play the audio again. Repeat if necessary for all students to complete the task.

track 1-36

IDEAS FOR... **Checking Comprehension**

Ask additional questions about the listening or write them on the board.

1. Which city is in the Murray-Darling Basin? (*Adelaide*)
2. Who did the government allocate most of the water to? (*to the city of Adelaide for domestic use and to big industrial farms*)
3. Why is it difficult to grow rice in Australia? (*because rice needs a lot of water*)

After Listening

Critical Thinking | Encourage students to evaluate the discussion from the audio and compare the information with their own opinions.

Answer Key

Answers will vary. Students' answers should include the main uses of water mentioned in the video: irrigation/agriculture; a habitat for fish/animals; to water gardens.

Pronunciation: Suffixes and Syllable Stress

 ■ Explain the meaning of *suffix* using this example: *A suffix can change the part of speech of a word such as from verb to noun.* Give some additional examples. Play the audio and ask students to repeat each word.

track 1-37

Exercise A.

track 1-38

Answer Key

1. in(dus)tri al 2. ag ri(cul)tur al 3. gov ern(men)tal 4. de(scrip)tion

Exercise B. | Encourage students to give each other feedback on syllable stress and pronunciation.

Exploring Spoken English
(pages 78-79)

Language Function: Expressing Opinions

- Read the information in the box.

- Ask students to complete each expression using their own ideas.

- Ask students for their opinions so they can reply using one of the expressions. For example:

  Q: Do you think long showers waste too much water?

  A: If you ask me, long showers waste water, and they aren't necessary.

  Q: What do you think about washing the dishes by hand to save water?

  A: I think dishwashers use less water, not more.

Exercise A.

- Look at the photos and discuss which of these activities uses the most water and which uses the least.

- Estimate how many times each one is used in a week and try to calculate the total water usage of an average household.

Exercise B. | Discussion

- Read the situation.

- Have students form groups and choose roles for themselves.

- Remind them to use language for expressing opinions and priorities.

- Appoint one person in each group to be the note-taker and another to be the spokesperson.

Exercise C.

- Encourage students to make a list of points from their discussion or to write them in a chart.

Exercise D. | Presentation

- Ask the spokesperson from each group to summarize their group's discussion for the rest of the class.

Grammar: Superlative Adjectives

- Go over the information in the box.

- You may also want to explain that adjectives ending with a consonant-vowel-consonant often double the final consonant for the superlative form (e.g., *big—biggest*). Point out that this does not affect pronunciation.

> **IDEAS FOR... Presenting Grammar**
>
> Dictate a short list of adjectives including both short and long adjectives. Ask students to say the superlative form for each one and then write them. Examples: *large, exciting, flat, wet, dry, wealthy, efficient, weak, strong*

Exercise A.

- Go over the answers as a class.

> **Answer Key**
>
> **1.** longest **2.** most poisonous **3.** most interesting
> **4.** tallest **5.** oldest **6.** best

Exercise B.

- Have students work individually. Then compare answers as a class.

> **Answer Key**
>
> **1.** The driest region in Australia is Western Australia.
> **2.** The most important crop in Australia is cotton.
> **3.** The biggest ocean is the Pacific Ocean.
> **4.** The heaviest land animal is the elephant.

> **TIP** This exercise includes two stages of correction. First, you can say if the sentence is formed correctly. Then you can say whether the sentence is factually correct.

Exercise C. | Discussion

- Have students work in pairs.

- Walk around the classroom to monitor their language usage.

Engage: Role-Playing a Meeting *(page 80)*

45 mins

WARM-UP

Explain that students are going to role play a government meeting to discuss how to allocate the local water supply. Discuss what kinds of language students will need to use. Some examples include agreeing and disagreeing, asking for and expressing opinions, and talking about priorities. Ask for examples of each type of language from this unit.

Exercise A.

■ Put students into groups of four and ask them to spend a few minutes reading the situation and the role cards. In their groups, they can assign one role to each member.

> **TIP** If groups don't divide evenly into groups of four, form one or more groups of five and add an extra role of a government facilitator who will ask additional questions to each organization.

Exercise B.

■ When they have chosen their roles, have students think carefully about "their" point of view about water use.

■ Have them make notes of arguments they can use in the meeting.

> **TIP** Another way of organizing this discussion is to have groups discuss one role each. Then mix up the groups so that one representative of each role is in each group.

Exercise C. | Role-Playing

■ Set a time limit for students to role play their meeting.

■ Walk around the classroom as students are speaking and take notes of useful expressions and ways of expressing opinions and priorities that you hear.

Presentation Skills: Speaking at the Right Volume | Go over the information in the box. Remind students to speak clearly and face the audience when addressing the class.

Exercise D. | Presentation

■ Before students start their presentations, you may want to discuss the criteria for evaluating a presentation. These could include clear organization, eye contact with audience, good posture, and appropriate speaking volume.

■ Students can use the criteria to evaluate each other's presentations.

> **TIP** You may decide to videotape these presentations for later discussion. This will help students evaluate and improve their performance.

> **IDEAS FOR... Expansion**
>
> For homework, ask students to research a country where water shortage is a problem and find out as much as they can about the country's water supply and usage. Why is there a shortage? What sorts of projects are under way to help? What are the problems? What are the possible solutions?

Inside the Brain

Academic Track
Health Science

Academic Pathways:
Lesson A: Listening to a Documentary
Discussing Problems and Solutions
Lesson B: Listening to a Conversation
between Students
Planning a Group Presentation

Unit Theme

This unit explores some interesting facts about the human brain. Although science has made many advances in understanding how the brain functions, much about the brain still remains a mystery.

Unit 5 explores the topic of the brain as it relates to:
– functions of different parts of the brain
– learning and memory
– emotions
– long-term and short-term memory

Think and Discuss *(page 81)*

5 mins

- Ask students to describe the photo. What information could scientists find out from this?

- Ask them if they would be willing to take part in scientific research about the brain.

Exploring the Theme: Inside the Brain *(pages 82-83)*

15 mins

The opening spread features a photo of a maze in England.

- Ask students to describe the photo and say what it has to do with the brain. Ask: *How can a maze be compared with a brain? How does the brain solve puzzles such as this maze?*

- Look at the smaller photos and read the captions. Ask: *What does Glen McNeill have to know in order to become a London cab driver? How is he learning it?*

- Discuss questions 1–3.

- Brainstorm ideas for question 1 and write them on the board (e.g., *solve problems, imagine stories, understand language, have feelings*).

- Discuss some general questions about whether everyone's brain is the same, how and why each one is different, and what affects the development of the brain.

IDEAS FOR... **Expansion**

Ask students to work in groups to complete a chart such as this one:

Things we know about the brain	Things we're not sure about	Things we would like to know

---

Building and Using Vocabulary *(pages 84-85)*

30 mins

WARM-UP

The Lesson A target vocabulary is presented in the context of facts about the brain.

- Ask students what they know about the brain. For example, ask what the different parts of the brain do and how the left side of the brain is different from the right side of the brain.

Building Vocabulary

track 2-2

Exercise A. | Meaning from Context

- Look at the photo and discuss what it might have to do with the brain.

- Play the audio while students read the text.

- Ask students which fact they found most interesting or surprising.

- Ask questions to check comprehension: *Why is it important to keep learning? What does the* hypothalamus *do? What do* neurons *do? What does the* amygdala *do?*

> **TIP** To make this exercise more challenging, you may want to play the audio with books closed and quiz students about the content.

Exercise B.

- Remind students to use the context to work out the meaning of these words.

Answer Key

1. generate	5. speeds	9. moods
2. signals	6. structure	10. connection
3. controls	7. tiny	
4. complex	8. function	

Using Vocabulary

Exercise A.

- Allow time for students to complete the sentences individually.

- Encourage students to try to remember the words without looking back at the definitions.

- Call on individual students to read their answers aloud.

Answer Key

1. function	5. tiny	9. connection
2. structure	6. signal	10. complex
3. speeds	7. mood	
4. generate	8. controls	

Exercise B. | Discussion

- Put students into pairs to discuss the questions.

- Discuss their answers as a class.

- Look at the photos and decide what moods these faces show and how you can tell. Discuss whether facial expressions have different meanings in different cultures.

> **TIP** Remind students to record new vocabulary in their vocabulary journals. Drawing a picture or diagram next to a word sometimes helps students remember the meaning.

Pronunciation Note

amygdala: uh-**mig**-duh-luh
hypothalamus: hahy-puh-**thal**-uh-muhs

Developing Listening Skills
(pages 86-87)

45 mins

Before Listening

Predicting Content

■ Look at the picture. Ask students what they think it shows. (*neural pathways*, *electrical activity*)

■ Ask which of the words in the box they think are likely to occur in the listening and in what context. For example, ask how exercise could affect the brain.

Listening: A Documentary

track 2-3 **Exercise A. |** Play the audio and check the answers from the previous exercise.

> **Answer Key**
>
> Exercise, neurons, learning, and memory are mentioned; food and intelligence are not mentioned.

track 2-3 **Exercise B. | Listening for Main Ideas**

■ Allow time for students to read the sentences.

■ Play the audio again while students choose their answers.

> **Answer Key**
>
> Your brain is a very important and complex organ.
> Your brain can send messages very quickly.

track 2-3 **Exercise C. | Listening for Details**

■ Allow time for students to read the sentences.

■ Play the audio again while students choose their answers.

■ Have students compare answers with each other before playing the audio again, if necessary, and checking the answers.

■ Ask students what facts they found most interesting or surprising in the documentary.

> **Answer Key**   1. F 2. F 3. F 4. T 5. T 6. T

> **IDEAS FOR...**   Checking Comprehension
>
> Ask students additional questions or write them on the board.
> 1. What does the story about the cat illustrate? (*how quickly your brain can process information*)
> 2. What do neurons do? (*They send messages around your brain.*)
> 3. What do motor neurons do? (*They tell parts of your body to move.*)
> 4. What does the story about the bike illustrate? (*how your brain changes when you learn new information*)

After Listening

Discussion

■ Ask students to work in pairs.

■ Encourage them to relate the documentary to their own experiences.

■ Help them compare and discuss their answers as a class.

Pronunciation: Linking Sounds
track 2-4

■ Read the information in the box.

■ Explain that linking words in this way will make them sound more fluent and natural.

■ Play the audio.

■ Say the sentences, emphasizing the linked words and ask students to repeat. Note: The link between *be* and *interesting* in the third example can be described as a /y/ sound.

Collaboration.
track 2-5

■ Play the audio again and pause so that students can repeat.

■ Go over the answers as a class.

■ Have students practice saying these sentences in pairs.

> **Answer Key**   2. C-V 3. C-SC 4. V-V 5. V-V 6. C-V

45 mins

Exploring Spoken English
(pages 88-90)

Grammar: Infinitives after Verbs

- Go over the information in the box.

- Explain the meaning of *transitive verbs* (verbs that take objects).

- You may want to note that some verbs can be transitive or intransitive. A good dictionary will show whether verbs are transitive (*T*) or intransitive (*I*) or both.

IDEAS FOR...   Presenting Grammar

Use the following activity to help students practice and remember verbs followed by infinitives. First, dictate the following sentences to students as they write them in their notebooks. Then students will walk around the classroom, asking questions to find the answers. Compare the answers as a class.

Find someone who . . .
   wants to learn something new.
   plans to take a vacation.
   hopes to go to college.
   has decided to get married.
   needs to save money.
   wants to learn a musical instrument.
   plans to go to a foreign country.
   needs to find a new job.
   hopes to meet someone new.

Exercise A.

- Read the questions aloud.

- Have students work in pairs to ask and answer the questions.

- Make a list of all the verbs on the board.

Exercise B.

- Allow time for students to complete the sentences individually.

- Invite volunteers to read their sentences aloud.

- Accept alternative answers.

Answer Key *(Answers may vary.)*

2. to help **3.** to brush **4.** to learn / to remember **5.** to buy **6.** to be / to feel **7.** to attend / to hear **8.** to see

---

Exercise C. | Discussion

- Put students into pairs to ask and answer the questions.

- Set a time limit to see who can come up with the most answers for each question within the given amount of time.

Exercise D.

- Look at the photos and read the captions.

- Ask students to come up with further questions or sentences about the pictures using verbs followed by infinitives.

Exercise E. | Self-Reflection

- Have students complete the sentences individually.

- Ask them to work with another student to compare and discuss their ideas.

- Ask one student from each pair to report the most interesting thing his or her partner said. (Remind them to say, *X plans to . . .*)

Exercise F.

- Model the exercise with a volunteer.

S: remember
T: I remembered to bring my lunch from home today.

Language Function: Making Suggestions

- Go over the information in the box.

- Present another problem situation and ask students to make suggestions. For example: *My computer has crashed and I don't know how to fix it.*

Exercise A.

- Put students in pairs to complete the conversation together and practice it, using expressions from the box.

Answer Key *(Answers may vary.)*

1. Why don't / Could **2.** could / could try to / might want to **3.** might **4.** Let's

Exercise B.

- Give students time to write their ideas.

- Have students work in pairs to discuss their situations and make suggestions.

> **IDEAS FOR...   Multi-level Classes**
>
> Students can decide how much they want to write in exercise **B**. Lower-level students may write just one sentence for each problem. Higher-level students can write a paragraph in their notebooks.

 TIP It may be uncomfortable for your students to talk about their personal problems. In this case, they can make up problems or talk about a friend or a relative.

> **IDEAS FOR...   Expansion**
>
> - Discuss where and how to get help and advice in your school or community.
> - Discuss the qualities of a good friend or counselor. (They listen to you, they empathize, they can think of various solutions.)

 # Speaking *(page 91)*

30-45 mins

Discussing Problems and Solutions

Exercise A.

- Call on volunteers to read each of the problems aloud to the class.

Exercise B. | Brainstorming

- Brainstorm a few ideas as a class for the first problem.

- Ask students to work individually to brainstorm ideas for the other problems.

- Have students present their ideas to the class.

- Make a list or a chart on the board to record the suggestions for each problem.

> **TIP** While students are discussing their problems, take notes on the expressions they use and any errors to mention when they have finished.

Exercise C.

- Ask three volunteers to read the examples in the speech bubbles.

- Explain that each person in the group will role play one of the people pictured on this page. The other group members will give suggestions and advice.

- Remind students to use the expressions from page 90.

> **TIP** If you are short of time, you can give each group a different problem to discuss.

Viewing: Memory Man

30 mins

(pages 92-93)

Overview of the Video | This video is about a man who has an amazing ability to remember.

Before Viewing

Exercise A. | Using a Dictionary

- Ask students to look at the photos and read the captions.

- Compare and contrast the two photos. How do they illustrate the terms *nature* and *nurture*?

- Ask students to use their dictionaries to look up new words.

- Ask them if they can think of any related words such as gene/genetic/genetics or heredity/inherit/inherited.

- Ask students to record these words in their vocabulary journals using new example sentences.

Exercise B. | Self-Reflection

- Encourage students to talk about what they can do well and whether they think these abilities were inherited or learned, or both.

While Viewing

Exercise A.

4:03

- Allow time for students to read the questions before watching the video.

- Play the video.

- Go over the answers as a class. Some students may have more answers than others.

Answer Key *(Answers may vary.)*

1. Italy **2.** see **3.** numbers, books, everything he learns, every detail of his life **4.** 11 **5.** his genes, continuous practice

Exercise B.

4:03

- Allow time for students to read the statements before watching the video again.

- Go over the answers as a class.

- Play the video (or parts of the video) again.

Answer Key   1. T 2. T 3. F 4. F 5. F 6. F

After Viewing

Exercise A. | Critical Thinking

- Ask students to give their own opinion and support it with the information they heard in the video.

> **IDEAS FOR...   Expansion**
>
> Ask students to discuss the question from three different points of view—Golfera's, a scientist's, a teacher's.

Exercise B.

- Set a time limit for this exercise and compare results with the whole class.

> **IDEAS FOR...   Expansion**
>
> You may want to try exercise **B** with words instead of numbers and see if there is any difference in how many items students can remember. If any students can remember all the numbers or all the words, ask them how they were able to do it and if they have any tips for improving memory.

Exercise C. | Discussion

- This exercise will help to prepare students for the next lesson. Ask them to support their opinions with reasons or examples.

Building and Using Vocabulary *(pages 94-95)*

WARM-UP

The Lesson B target vocabulary is presented in the context of research on love and affection.

- Ask students if they think there are different types of love. What are they? What is the difference between love, affection, and friendship?

Building Vocabulary

Exercise A. | Prior Knowledge

- Ask students to think of some people they love. Why do they love them?

- Brainstorm ideas for what attracts you to certain types of people.

Exercise B. | Meaning from Context

track 2-6

- Look at the photo and the title and ask students to predict the content.

- Play the audio while students read.

> **IDEAS FOR...** Checking Comprehension
>
> Ask students to choose one statement from the article and explain why they agree or disagree with it by giving additional arguments.

Using Vocabulary

Critical Thinking Focus: Using Context Clues

- Go over the information in the box.

- Explain that these are three different kinds of context clues that can help you when you don't understand a word.

Exercise A.

- Ask students to work in pairs, look back at the article, and find one additional example of each type of clue.

Exercise B.

- Encourage students to discuss all the blue words from the passage and decide what kind of context clues they can use to figure out their meanings.

- The answers below are examples. Accept any reasonable answers that students can explain.

> **Answer Key** *(Answers may vary.)*
>
> Definition:
> . . . **short-term** condition. <u>With time, strong, romantic feelings decrease . . .</u>
> (short-term = something that continues for a short time)
>
> . . . levels of **oxytocin**—<u>a brain chemical connected with calm feelings of happiness and trust.</u>
> (oxytocin = a brain chemical that helps your mood)
>
> Other words nearby:
> Your brain knows the difference between **romantic** love and other attachments. When we're <u>in love,</u> . . .
> (romantic = associated with being in love)
>
> Knowledge of the world:
> . . . <u>while chemicals do affect the</u> <u>way we feel,</u> **psychological** <u>factors are also important</u>.
> (I know that people's thoughts and experiences contribute to falling in love, not just chemicals, so psychological = having to do with thoughts and experiences)

Exercise C.

- Have students complete the exercise individually.

- Ask them to work in groups to compare their answers.

> **Answer Key**
>
> | | | |
> |---|---|---|
> | 1. long-term | 5. emotions | 9. short-term |
> | 2. similar | 6. function | 10. security |
> | 3. attachment | 7. psychological | |
> | 4. concentrate | 8. romantic | |

TIP Remind students to record these new words in their vocabulary journals using example sentences and/or synonyms to help them remember their meanings.

Developing Listening Skills

45 mins *(pages 96-97)*

Before Listening

 Exercise A.
track 2-7

- Explain that students will listen to classmates talking about a lecture.

- Play the audio while students read.

- Ask what they think the main topic is. (*short-term memory*)

- Ask what students know about short-term memory and if they can think of any examples.

Exercise B. | Understanding Visuals

- Refer to page 215 of the *Independent Student Handbook* for another version of a flow chart.

- Have students work in pairs to discuss the questions.

- Discuss the answers as a class. Ask for some examples of things that students remember really well such as a happy event from their childhood.

Listening: A Conversation between Students

 Exercise A. | Listening for Main Ideas
track 2-8

- Explain to students that the audio is a discussion among three people. They heard the beginning of the discussion in Before Listening on page 96.

- Tell students to listen for the people's conclusions about long-term and short-term memory.

- Play the audio while students take notes.

- Go over the answers with the whole class.

Answer Key *(Answers may vary.)*

Short-term memory: A process that lets you easily remember something, such as a question, long enough to function normally. It only lasts a few seconds.

Long-term memory: A process for remembering something important. You have to work to remember it, and the memory lasts much longer. You need to really concentrate to remember it.

Exercise B. | Listening for Details

- Allow time for students to read the beginning of each sentence.

- Play the audio again.

- Invite students to write their answers on the board.

Answer Key

1. decide that something is important

2. concentrate / focus

3. do it again and again

IDEAS FOR... **Checking Comprehension**

Ask students additional questions or write them on the board.
1. How long does short-term memory last? (*a few seconds*)
2. What is an example of short-term memory? (*remembering a question so that you can answer it*)

After Listening

Exercise A.

- Ask students to report the most interesting points in their discussion to the class.

- Discuss ways to move things from short-term memory into long-term memory.

Exercise B. | Self-Reflection

- Allow time for students to complete their answers individually.

Exercise C. | Discussion

- Explain that reflecting on your learning and memory is a good way of improving your memory skills.

IDEAS FOR... **Expansion**

Encourage students to collect tips on how to remember new vocabulary. Post the tips on a notice board or class Web site to share with other students.

Exploring Spoken English
(pages 98-99)

Exercise A. | Self-Reflection

- Look at the photo and describe what the people are doing. Possible verbs you might use include *listening, discussing, planning, agreeing, disagreeing, negotiating,* and *cooperating.*

- Invite students to discuss what they enjoy or dislike about group work. Ask: *Why is it important? What does it help you to learn?*

Exercise B. | Brainstorming

- Discuss one or two advantages or disadvantages as a class.

- Allow time for students to work in pairs to complete the chart.

- Invite volunteers to write their ideas in a chart on the board.

Exercise C. | Critical Thinking

- Discuss one of the disadvantages as a class and suggest ways to solve it.

- Have students continue the discussion in pairs.

Exercise D. | Discussion

- Go over the expressions in the Language Function box.

- Ask each pair to join up with another pair to compare their ideas.

Language Function: Making Suggestions during Group Work

- Go over the expressions in this box before doing exercise **D** above.

- Present a situation where students have to do a survey of opinions about group work. Ask for their suggestions on how to carry out the survey using the expressions in the box.

Student to Student: Presenting Your Ideas in a Small Group

- Read the information in the box and remind students to use this language in exercise **D**.

Exercise A.

- Read the assignment aloud.

- Ask some comprehension questions about the information: *How many researchers are mentioned? Which researcher studied monkeys?*

Exercise B. | Critical Thinking

- Point out that each person pictured has a different point of view and thus different preferences about the assignment.

- Remind them to read the information carefully and reread the assignment if necessary.

- Allow time for groups to discuss and complete the missing expressions.

- Check the answers by nominating students to read their answers out loud and asking if the rest of the class agrees.

Answer Key *(Answers may vary.)*

Olivier: Bowlby

Ebadi: Can / Why don't

Chang: suggest

Santos: Harlow, Bowlby

Day: Let's / I suggest we, Shaver / Bowlby

Baldari: Why don't / Can

IDEAS FOR... **Expansion**

In groups of six, have each student role play one of the people on this page. As a group, they should first decide which researchers to select. Then they decide who will present each part of the presentation, who will prepare the visuals, and who will introduce the presentation. While they are doing this, monitor their discussions to see if they are using the target phrases correctly. At the end of the activity, you may want to ask students to reflect on the importance of using the expressions in order to cooperate successfully with group members.

Engage: Planning a Group Presentation *(page 100)*

45 mins

WARM-UP

Explain that students are going to work together in a group to plan a presentation. Ask students what role they prefer to take in group work and what they feel they are best at.

Exercise A.

- Put students into groups of four.

- Read the information about group roles and make sure every student understands his or her role. Assign roles or ask students to select their own role.

> **TIP** If you have extra students, make one or more groups of five and give the extra role of *coach*, which is described in the *Independent Student Handbook* on page 211.

Exercise B. | Planning a Presentation Allow time for groups to choose their topics. Make sure all topics are covered. Make sure all students are carrying out their roles.

Exercise C. | Discussion

- Explain that the questions will help students to start thinking about how to plan their presentation.

- Encourage students to think of different ways to research their topics. You may want to discuss different ways to search the Web, and ways to find interesting visuals. It could also be helpful to think of different ways to practice their presentations. They could record their presentations using an online resource, for example.

- Remind students to use language for making suggestions from page 98.

- Make sure students are carrying out their roles.

Exercise D. | Organizing Ideas

- Encourage students to practice reporting to their group. One person can introduce the topic and say why they chose it. Each person should have an equal amount to say.

Exercise E. | Reporting to the Class

- Encourage students to take turns reporting their group's ideas.

> **TIP** Ask students to reflect on how they felt about working in a group and compare it with their ideas from page 98.

Exercise F. | Presentation

- Give students a date by which their presentation should be ready. You may want to spread the presentations over two or three classes.

> **TIP** Walk around the classroom as students are speaking and take notes of other useful strategies that students are using to agree, disagree, negotiate, and discuss.

Presentation Skills: Pausing to Check Understanding | Read the information in the box. Remind students to pause frequently when addressing the whole class. Pauses help listeners process ideas, and they also give the speaker a chance to see what the audience response is like.

What We Eat

Academic Track
Health and Nutrition

Academic Pathways:
Lesson A: Listening to a Seminar
Participating in a Mini-Debate
Lesson B: Listening to a Group Discussion
Using Visuals to Support
a Presentation

Unit Theme

This unit explores some interesting facts about food and diet. Eating habits are changing in many countries, and it is important to be aware of the effects of these changes on health.

Unit 6 explores the topic of food as it relates to:
– healthy eating
– changes in eating habits
– food in Mexico

– dietary guidelines
– fast food

Think and Discuss *(page 101)*

5 mins

- Ask students to describe the photo.

- Ask students the following questions: *How is this type of farming similar or different to farming in your country? Are there many small farms in your country? What other types of crops are grown in different regions of the world?* Make a list of different staple crops (e.g., rice, wheat, corn) and where each one is grown.

Exploring the Theme: What We Eat *(pages 102-103)*

15 mins

The opening spread features a photo of rice field terraces in China.

- Ask students to describe the photo. How is the landscape similar to or different from other countries they know? What do they think might be the problems or advantages of this type of farming?

Exercise A.

- Look at the food diagram. Have students identify all the foods in each section.

- Read the information and discuss questions 1 and 2. Explain the meaning of the word *serving* (amount of food that is enough for one person).

- You may want to bring in a similar diagram from the United States or have students bring in one from their country to compare.

Exercise B.

- Have students look at the smaller photos and read the captions.

- Discuss questions 1–3.

- Ask students to describe the average diet in their country.

- Ask students how much a family of four would spend on food each week in the area where they are from.

> **IDEAS FOR... Expansion**
>
> Ask students to work in pairs to create a food chart similar to the one on page 103 for their own typical weekly diet. What percentage of their diet is fruit, vegetables, meat, etc.? Ask students to compare charts with other pairs of students.

Building and Using Vocabulary *(pages 104-105)*

30 mins

WARM-UP

The Lesson A target vocabulary is presented in the context of information about food and nutrition.

- Ask students what they think are the healthiest foods.

- Discuss whether they think diet is the most important factor in staying healthy, or if other factors are more important.

Building Vocabulary

Exercise A. | Using a Dictionary

- Ask students to look at the photo and name the vegetables and fruits they recognize.

- Encourage students to make sentences with the words in the box. They can use a dictionary to check if their usage is correct.

> **TIP** You may want to help students identify which words are verbs, nouns, or adjectives. This will help them with exercise B.

Exercise B.

- Do the first sentence with the class as an example.

- Set a time limit for students to complete the sentences.

Answer Key

1. guidelines	5. source	9. specific
2. recommend	6. regional	10. average
3. vitamins	7. include	
4. servings	8. improve	

Exercise C.

track 2-9

- Ask volunteers to write their answers on the board.

- Play the audio for students to check their answers.

- If appropriate, help students with pronunciation of the target words.

IDEAS FOR... Multi-level Classes

To make the exercises on page 104 more challenging, suggest students choose one of the following options:

1. Complete exercise **B** according to the directions.
2. Listen to the sentences in Track **2-9** without reading along in exercise **B**, and write which vocabulary words they hear for each sentence.

Exercise D.

- Remind students to look back at exercise **B** and use the context to work out the answers.

> **TIP** Explain that context is important in determining the meaning of a word, and the meaning of the word in a particular context may not always match its dictionary definition.

Answer Key

1. normal	5. suggest	9. particular
2. rules	6. local	10. substances
3. make better	7. amount	
4. contain	8. cause	

Using Vocabulary

Exercise A. | Self-Reflection

- Discuss ways that we can make our diet healthy.

- Do the first item as an example. *I eat five servings of fruit and vegetables every day.*

- Allow time for students to complete their answers individually.

- Make sure students write sentences that are relevant.

Exercise B. | Discussion

- Put students into pairs to discuss their answers.

- Call on volunteers to read one or two of their answers aloud.

- Ask the class if they agree with the volunteers' explanation or example.

Exercise C. | Critical Thinking

- Ask students to discuss the questions in pairs and summarize the main points of their discussion for the class.

Developing Listening Skills

(pages 106-107)

Pronunciation: Intonation of Finished and Unfinished Sentences

track 2-10

- Play the audio and ask students to repeat the examples.

- Mention that it is often considered impolite to interrupt before a speaker has finished. Students will learn about polite ways of interrupting later in the lesson on page 109.

track 2-11

Exercise A.

- Play the audio and go over the answers.

> **Answer Key**   1. F 2. U 3. U 4. F 5. U 6. F

Exercise B.

- Tell students to practice the intonation patterns in pairs. They can also make up their own examples.

Before Listening

Discussion

- Discuss possible meanings of *modernization* with the class. Brainstorm ideas and write them on the board. Possible ideas include new technology, better living conditions, more cars, machines, and factories.

Listening: A Seminar

track 2-12

Exercise A. | Listening for Main Ideas

- Read the information in the box above exercise **A**. Ask about students' experience of attending seminars.

- Read the three questions and ask students to predict what changes there might have been in the Korean diet.

- Play the first part of the audio and check the answers.

> **Answer Key**
>
> 1. changes in the Korean diet
> 2. People eat more food—less rice, but more vegetables, fruit, meat, and dairy products.
> 3. 1995

track 2-12

Exercise B. | Listening for Details

- Play the first part of the audio again while students complete the chart.

> **Answer Key**
>
> Total Food: 37, 39
> Rice and Grain: 20, 11
> Vegetables: 9.5, 10
> Fruit: 2, 5
> Meat: 0.25, 2.5
> Milk and Dairy Products: 0.1, 2.3

track 2-13

Exercise C.

- Read the questions aloud.

- Play the second part of the audio while students take notes.

- Ask students to discuss the questions in pairs.

- Invite volunteers to write the answers in a chart on the board.

> **Answer Key**
>
> 1. They eat more animal products.
> 2. They are taller.
> 3. a. The modern diet in Korea is healthier than the traditional diet.

IDEAS FOR... **Checking Comprehension**

Ask these additional questions or write them on the board.

1. What was Korea like 50 years ago (according to the speaker)? *(an agricultural country)*
2. Describe a traditional Korean diet. *(mainly rice and vegetables and not much fruit, meat, or dairy)*
3. Describe a modern Korean diet. *(less rice and more fruit, meat, and dairy)*

After Listening

Discussion

- Encourage students to relate the information to their own knowledge and experience.

- Discuss the answers as a class.

45 mins

Exploring Spoken English
(pages 108-110)

Grammar: The Real Conditional with the Present

- Go over the information in the box.

- Practice reversing the clauses in each sentence. For example: *Children grow up to be taller if they eat more protein.*

Exercise A.

- Read the first example aloud.

- Have students work individually to complete the sentences.

- Discuss the answers as a class.

> **Answer Key** *(Answers may vary.)*
>
> 2. If you don't sleep enough, you feel tired. / You feel tired if you don't sleep enough.
>
> 3. If you use less electricity, you save money. / You save money if you use less electricity.
>
> 4. If you don't eat a healthy diet, you get sick. / You get sick if you don't eat a healthy diet.
>
> 5. If you don't water a plant, it dies. / A plant dies if you don't water it.
>
> 6. If you don't drink enough water on a hot day, you feel thirsty. / You feel thirsty if you don't drink enough water on a hot day.

Exercise B.

- Students can ask each other questions using the prompts. For example: *What happens if you eat a lot of sugar?*

- Set a time limit to see who can come up with the most answers for each question.

- Invite volunteers to tell the class one of their answers.

- Ask for alternative answers for each situation.

> **TIP** In exercise B, give feedback on both the grammatical form and the content of the answer, as appropriate.

Exercise C. | Self-Reflection

- Have students work individually to write their answers.

Exercise D. | Discussion

- Tell students to work in pairs to find out how many of their ideas were the same.

- Ask volunteers to tell the class their partner's most interesting idea.

Language Function: Interrupting and Returning to Topic

- Read the information in the box.

- Ask students to write a short conversation using two examples from the box.

- Ask volunteers to read their conversations to the class.

Exercise A.

- Discuss the photo. Ask who is speaking and who is interrupting.

- Remind students that this language function was used in the presentation on page 107 and play the audio again if appropriate.

- Read the sentences aloud. Discuss who said each sentence.

> **IDEAS FOR...** **Presenting Grammar**
>
> Use the following activity to help students review the real conditional with the present.
>
> Prepare one piece of paper for each pair of students. Each paper will have a different sentence starter at the top of the page (see examples below). Each pair writes one clause to finish the sentence and passes it on to the next pair. Every pair writes a new clause that must be different from the ones already on the paper.
>
> If I feel depressed, I . . .
>
> If I feel happy, I . . .
>
> If I want to study, I . . .
>
> If I want to feel peaceful, I . . .
>
> If I have a problem, I . . .
>
> If I need help with my homework, I . . .
>
> Ask volunteers to read some of the best answers aloud.

Exercise B.

- To check students' answers, read the expressions from exercise **A** aloud. Ask students which column each expression should go in and write the answers on the board.

Answer Key

Stopping a Speaker	Going Back to the Topic
Can/Could/May I interrupt? Can I stop you for a second? May I say something here? Could I ask a question?	Anyway, . . . Moving on, . . . As I was saying, . . . To continue, . . .
Other ideas: I'd like to ask a question, if I may. Excuse me, could you please explain . . . ?	Other ideas: To get back to the topic, . . .

Exercise C. | Role-Playing

- Read the situation aloud and go over the instructions with students.

- Ask one student to summarize the instructions.

- Set a time limit for students to write their ideas.

- Remind students to use the expressions from exercise **B** in their discussion.

> **TIP** It may be helpful to brainstorm a few general topic areas to help students get started such as snacks, chips, soft drinks, coffee, fried food, fruit, and vegetables.

Exercise D. | Presentation

- Encourage other students to respond to each group's guidelines by asking questions.

Exercise E. | Discussion

- Discuss cultural differences of social rules for interrupting. Does it depend where you are or who you are speaking to?

> **TIP** If students do not have direct experience with American culture, you may ask them to compare their country with another country they know well.

Speaking (page 111)

30-45 mins

Participating in a Mini-Debate

Exercise A. | Planning a Presentation

- Have students work in pairs.

- Tell each pair to agree or disagree with the given statement so that there are equal numbers of students on each side of the argument.

Exercise B. | Brainstorming

- Go over the information in the box.

- Ask students to think of a reason and an explanation in favor of a traditional diet.

- Set a time limit for pairs to write their ideas.

Exercise C.

- While students are writing, walk around the classroom and check their work to make sure they understand the difference between a reason and a supporting example.

Exercises D, E, and F.

- In these three exercises, students first listen to a pair of students with the opposing point of view and take notes. Then they think of arguments to counter the opposing pair's reasons, explanations, and examples. After they have come up with their arguments, they meet up with the opposing pair again. Emphasize that this activity is like a competitive debate between debate teams—they don't necessarily give their real opinions.

Exercise D. | Note-Taking

- Encourage students to listen carefully at this stage. They should not respond to their opponents yet.

Exercise E. | Critical Thinking.

- Encourage students to develop their arguments before returning to their group.

Exercise F.

- Tell students to return to their group and present their arguments.

> **TIP** Remind students to use language for interrupting politely and returning to a topic.

Viewing: The Food and Culture of Oaxaca

30 mins

(pages 112-113)

Overview of the Video | This video is about the traditional culture of the city and state of Oaxaca in Mexico, with particular focus on its food.

Before Viewing

Exercise A. | Prior Knowledge

- Ask students to look at the photos and read the captions.

- Discuss what is happening in the second photo. (*She is making tortillas and toasting chilies. There is a fire under the large clay plate.*) Ask students if they are interested in cooking. Have them tell you why or why not.

- Discuss what kinds of Mexican food they have tried and whether they like them.

Exercise B. | Predicting Content

- Write all the words students come up with on the board.

While Viewing

Exercise A. | Checking Predictions
2:46
- Play the video and circle any words on the board from the previous exercise that are mentioned.

Exercise B. | Note-Taking
2:46
- Play the video again.

- Have students discuss their answers in pairs before going over the exercise as a class.

Answer Key *(Answers may vary.)*

chilies / chili peppers, *mole* / a sauce called *mole*, spices, chicken, meat

Exercise C.

- Tell students to work in pairs.

- Invite volunteers to call out their answers. To turn this exercise into a competition, keep track of who gets the most words.

Exercise D.
2:46
- Allow time for students to read the sentences before watching the video again.

- Play the video again.

- Check the answers as a class.

Answer Key   1. T 2. F 3. F 4. T 5. T 6. F

Exercise E.
2:46
- Ask students to complete the sentences.

- Play the video again.

Answer Key

1. colors, smells 2. famous 3. loves 4. learn, dishes
5. heard, countries 6. interesting, difficult 7. happy, eat

After Viewing

Exercise A.

- Encourage students to think about the information in the video and relate it to their own experience.

Exercise B. | Conditional Sentences

- Set a time limit for this exercise and go over the answers as a class.

Answer Key   1. d 2. a 3. c 4. b

Exercise C. | Using a Graphic Organizer

- Explain that this exercise will help students prepare for the next lesson.

IDEAS FOR...   Expansion

Use this type of graphic organizer to brainstorm ideas about other food-related contrasts, such as being a vegetarian vs. eating meat and fish, eating rice vs. wheat or corn, and so on. This will help students understand the benefits of using a graphic organizer to gather ideas before attending a lecture or seminar, or before writing an essay.

Pronunciation Note
Oaxaca: wuh-**hah**-kuh
Mole: **moh**-ley
Guelaguetza: gway-la-**get**-za

30 mins

Building and Using Vocabulary *(pages 114-115)*

WARM-UP

The Lesson B target vocabulary is presented in the context of visual graphics to represent information about food and nutrition.

- Ask students what kind of graphic organizers they use in their note-taking. Refer students to pages 214–215 in the *Independent Student Handbook*.

Building Vocabulary

Exercise A. | Meaning from Context
track 2-14

- Discuss the four visuals as a class before reading the text.

- Assign one visual to each group of students and ask them to prepare an explanation of what it shows. Each group can present their explanation to the class.

- Have students work independently to look at the descriptions and match them to the visuals.

Answer Key   1. b 2. a 3. d 4. c

IDEAS FOR...   Checking Comprehension

After checking answers, ask additional questions about the charts and diagrams.
a. What period of time does the line graph cover? When was the lowest consumption of sugar?
b. Which age group eats the most fruit? How many servings of fruit do teenagers eat?
c. What categories of food are shown in the diagram? Which category has the highest number of servings?
d. What are some examples of food from each section of the pie chart? Why are some sections bigger than others?

Exercise B. | Self-Reflection

- Ask students to work in pairs to discuss which of the charts and diagrams most accurately reflect the eating patterns and money spent on food in their countries.

Using Vocabulary

Exercise A.

- Allow time for students to write their answers.

- Point out the arrows in items 2 and 9.

- Tell students to check their answers in pairs and tell you if they disagree about any of them.

Answer Key

1. point   5. label   9. x axis
2. section   6. pie chart   10. diagram
3. bar graph   7. line graph
4. line   8. represents

Exercise B. | Understanding Visuals

- Tell students to relate these definitions to the longer explanations on page 114.

Answer Key   1. a 2. c 3. b 4. d

Exercise C.

- Have students work in pairs to decide which type of visual to use.

- Recommend that students turn to page 216 of the *Independent Student Handbook* for good descriptions of what each type of visual is for.

Answer Key   1. bar graph 2. line graph
3. pie chart 4. bar graph

TIP   If your class has computers available for use, help students access tools for creating these types of charts.

IDEAS FOR...   Expansion

Discuss how you might find out the information for the topics in exercise **B** (how people eat and spend money on food in different countries). Ask students to choose one of the topics, or another topic related to food, and do some research that they can present in the form of a chart or graph.

Developing Listening Skills

45 mins *(pages 116-117)*

Before Listening

Exercise A. | Discussion

- Elicit students' opinions about fast food. Ask a few questions: *Does fast food taste good or bad? Why is it so popular?*

- Tell students that the pictures show fast foods that are favorites in the United States.

- Ask students about popular fast foods in other countries they know of.

Exercise B.

- Explain that the assignment is for a group of students and that the group will be discussing it on the audio.

- Choose a student to read the assignment aloud to the class.

- Ask some questions to check comprehension: *What is the topic of the presentation? How will it be presented?*

- Have students discuss the two questions in pairs.

Listening: A Group Discussion

 track 2-15 **Exercise A. | Listening for Main Ideas**

- Look at the photo and discuss what these people are doing. Who are they and why did they choose this restaurant?

- Read the sentences and explain that students will hear a group discussion. They have to do two things: check the ideas they hear and then circle the one that the students on the audio finally choose.

- Play the audio.

Answer Key

✓ make a list of fast food restaurants that have healthy choices
✓ tell people how often it's OK to eat fast food

 track 2-16 **Exercise B. | Listening for Details**

- Allow time for students to read the sentences.

- Play the second part of the audio.

Answer Key   1. F 2. T 3. T 4. T 5. F 6. T

 track 2-17 **Exercise C.**

- Play the third part of the audio (sentences from the previous discussion). Go over the answers as a class.

Exercise D.

- Play the audio and pause after each sentence for students to repeat before asking students to practice in pairs.

Answer Key   1. No 2. Yes 3. Yes 4. Yes 5. No

IDEAS FOR...   Checking Comprehension

Ask these additional questions or write them on the board.
1. How often does the average person in the United States eat fast food? (*twice a week*)
2. What does "You're kidding!" mean? (*You're joking. / That's surprising.*)
3. What are two ways of interpreting the word "occasionally"? (*One student says once a week; the others say once a month.*)

After Listening

- Encourage students to think creatively and give positive feedback for original ideas.

IDEAS FOR...   Expansion

Before your students begin their discussion, play Track 2-16 again. Have students listen for short expressions that are used to keep the discussion flowing smoothly. Put the expressions on the board and have students write them in their notebooks: *Great! You're right! I know. That's a great idea. No problem.*

Have students use the expressions in their own discussions.

Exploring Spoken English
(pages 118-119)

Language Function: Managing a Discussion

- Go over the information in the box.
- Point out that it addresses a common difficulty when working in a group—completing the work correctly and on time.

Exercise A.

- Tell students that the expressions are from the student discussions they heard on page 117.
- Ask one student to read the questions and another to read the statements aloud.
- Allow time for students to work on the exercise individually.
- Check the answers as a class.
- Ask for suggestions for other expressions that could express these functions.

Answer Key	1. e 2. d 3. b 4. a 5. f 6. c

Exercise B.

- Explain that these are diet guidelines from three different countries, presented in diagrams.
- Ask students to work in groups. First, have them choose the diet they think is the healthiest. Then have them choose the clearest, most effective diagram.
- Suggest that each person in the group use at least three expressions from exercise **A**.
- At the end of the discussion, ask a spokesperson for each group to summarize the group's decision and explain it to the class.

Grammar: The Real Conditional with the Future

- Go over the information in the box.
- Explain the sequence of tenses in this structure. (The *if* clause uses the present tense. The main clause uses the future with *will*.)

- You may want to contrast this with the real conditional with the present, which was presented on page 108.

Exercise A.

- Allow time for students to write their answers individually.
- Ask volunteers to read their answers aloud.

Answer Key

1. eat, won't be able to
2. exercise, will lose/ 'll lose
3. don't get, you will be/ you'll be
4. won't be, have
5. don't have, won't be able to
6. don't eat, will feel / 'll feel

Exercise B. | Discussion

- An alternative way of using this exercise is to divide the class into groups. Give one topic to each group to discuss. Ask them to present their ideas to the class.

IDEAS FOR... **Presenting Grammar**

Prepare a set of real conditional sentences with the future and cut them into two halves. Give one half to each student. Ask them to walk around the classroom and find their partner.

Here are some examples:
If you drink coffee, you'll stay awake longer.
If you eat chocolate, you won't feel tired.
You won't get high blood pressure if you eat less salt.
If you give up coffee, you'll sleep better.
You'll save money if you don't eat meat.
If you eat more vegetables, you'll feel healthier.
If you eat less ice cream, you'll lose weight.

When all the clauses are paired, have students read them aloud. Ask if they agree or disagree with the statements produced.

Engage: Using Visuals to Support a Presentation

(page 120)

45 mins

WARM-UP

Read the information in the box aloud. Ask students for their ideas about how children's guidelines might differ from adults' and ask what kind of visuals would appeal to children.

Exercise A.

- Explain that students are going to work together in a group to prepare a presentation using visuals. Remind them of the different types of visuals you have studied in this unit.

- Put students into pairs or groups of three. Ask a student to read the situation aloud.

- Ask some questions to check comprehension: What are the guidelines about? (*healthy eating for children 4–8 years old*) Who are they for? (*guidelines for parents; visuals for children*)

- Read the instructions for steps 1, 2, and 3 aloud. Explain that in step 1, students prepare written guidelines and visuals using the information in the chart.

- Go over the chart. You may want to mention that dairy products are a good source of protein, and that vegetarian foods such as beans, lentils, and tofu are protein sources as well.

- Remind students of expressions they learned in this unit for managing a group discussion (pages 110 and 118).

- Go over the Student to Student box as described below.

- Set a time limit for students to work together.

Student to Student: Expressing Thanks and Appreciation

- Read the information in the box aloud.

- You may want to mention that *I really appreciate your making that chart* is grammatically correct and some people prefer it; *I really appreciate you making that chart* is also acceptable.

TIP Walk around the classroom as students are working together and note language strategies that they are using to manage their discussions. Mention them when students finish.

Exercise B. | Planning a Presentation

- Tell students the amount of time they will have for giving their presentations. (Between four and six minutes should be enough.)

- Tell students when they will make their presentations—the same day or at a later time.

- Go over the expressions in the Presentation Skills box as described below.

- Tell students the criteria for assessing these presentations such as speaking clearly, making eye contact with the audience, pausing frequently, and using appropriate language for talking about their visuals.

- Emphasize the importance of practicing a presentation before giving it in front of an audience. If possible, allow class time for students to practice their presentations in pairs.

Presentation Skills: Talking about Visuals

- Go over the information in the box.

- Refer back to the diagrams on page 118 and let students practice using these phrases to talk about them.

- Remind students to use these phrases when presenting their visuals in exercise **C**.

Exercise C. | Presentation

- Remind students of the time limit and the criteria for assessing each presentation.

- You may want to assign students to keep time and give them the responsibility of warning groups when they have one minute left.

- Remember to allow time for interruptions and follow-up questions and answers.

- Remind students to use language for talking about visuals from the box.

Our Active Earth

Academic Track
Earth Science

Academic Pathways:
Lesson A: **Listening to an Earth**
Science Lecture
Giving a News Report
Lesson B: **Listening to a Group Discussion**
Giving a Group Presentation

Unit Theme

This unit explores some interesting facts about earthquakes and volcanoes. Natural disasters are a fascinating topic of scientific interest, but they are also very dangerous and cause a great deal of damage.

Unit 7 explores the topic of nature as it relates to:
– buildings that are able to withstand earthquakes
– the causes of earthquakes
– what to do in an earthquake
– volcanoes

Think and Discuss *(page 121)*

5 mins

- Ask students to describe the photo.

- Discuss the questions.

Answer Key *(Answers will vary.)*

Possible answer for 1: Both involve movements in the earth's crust. Possible answer for 2: Indonesia and Chile are two countries that have volcanoes.

Exploring the Theme:
Our Active Earth *(pages 122-123)*

15 mins

The opening spread features a photo of a volcanic eruption.

- Ask students to describe the photo. You may want to pre-teach the words *erupt* and *lava*.

- Ask students if they have ever visited a volcano. If they have, ask them to tell the class about it.

Exercise A.

- Ask students to look at the diagrams and read the information.

- Discuss questions 1 and 2. How are earthquakes and volcanic eruptions similar and different?

Exercise B.

- Look at the map and go over the information.

- Discuss questions 1–3.

- Ask students what they know about recent volcanic eruptions or earthquakes in the world.

> **IDEAS FOR... Expansion**
>
> - Ask students to write a list of things they would like to learn about volcanoes and earthquakes. Then have students choose the three most interesting questions and research them for homework.
> - Have students brainstorm adjectives, verbs, and nouns to describe the photo and use them to write a poem about volcanoes.

Building and Using Vocabulary *(pages 124-125)*

30 mins

WARM-UP

The Lesson A target vocabulary is presented in the context of information about destruction that can be caused by earthquakes.

- Ask students what they think causes the most destruction during an earthquake.

- Ask students if they remember any details about recent volcanic eruptions or earthquakes in the news.

Building Vocabulary

track 2-18

Exercise A. | Meaning from Context

- Look at the title of the article with students and ask what the text could be about.

- Play the audio while students read.

- Ask students to suggest alternative words for the words in blue.

> **IDEAS FOR...** **Checking Comprehension**
>
> Ask students to summarize the main ideas of the text by answering these questions:
> *How are earthquakes caused?*
> *Why did more people die in Haiti than in Chile?*

Using Vocabulary

Exercise B. | Discussion

- Ask questions about the information in the diagrams. Ask which countries' buildings have lightweight walls, which have heavy, reinforced walls, which have heavy, non-reinforced walls, and so on.

- Ask students to give reasons for their answers to these questions.

Exercise C.

- Encourage students to try to remember the words before looking back at the text.

- Point out that two words from exercise **A** are not used.

> **Answer Key** *(Answers may vary.)*
>
> **1.** collapse **2.** reinforce/construct **3.** survive
> **4.** shakes **5.** dangerous **6.** materials **7.** push **8.** be killed

Exercise D. | Critical Thinking

- Remind students to use vocabulary from the previous exercise in their discussions.

> **IDEAS FOR...** **Multi-level Classes**
>
> In exercise **D**, ask students to think of as many answers as possible for the questions. When you gather ideas from the class, ask lower-level students first so that higher-level students have to come up with additional, less obvious answers.

> **IDEAS FOR...** **Expansion**
>
> Ask students to describe the typical construction of buildings in their city or country. It may be helpful to bring in some pictures of different types of construction and compare them.

Developing Listening Skills

(pages 126-127)

Before Listening

- Have students look at the picture and predict what the listening will be about.

- Read the text together and label the places in the picture. Write the answers on the board.

Answer Key

1. mountains in Iran 2. Eurasian Plate 3. Arabian Plate
4. Persian Gulf 5. Gulf of Oman

Listening: An Earth Science Lecture

Exercise A. | Listening for Main Ideas

- Read the questions aloud. Play the first part of the audio while students take notes. Go over the answers as a class.

Answer Key *(Answers may vary.)*

1. plate tectonics 2. 14 3. divergent (convergent to form mountains in Iran) 4. rough

Exercise B.

- Help students to interpret the chart.

- Ask students to fill in any information they remember before listening to the audio again.

Exercise C. | Note-Taking

- Play the audio again while students take notes. Invite volunteers to write their answers in a chart on the board.

Answer Key *(Answers may vary.)*

Border Type: Divergent

Movement: Plates move past each other.

Results: Mountains are formed.

IDEAS FOR... Checking Comprehension

Ask these additional questions or write them on the board.

1. How many major plates are there? (*14*)
2. What is one example of a convergent boundary? (*the Himalayas*)
3. What is one example of a divergent boundary? (*the Persian Gulf*)
4. What is one example of a transform boundary? (*the San Andreas Fault in California and northern Mexico*)

After Listening

Critical Thinking Focus: Predicting Exam Questions

- Go over the information in the box.

- Ask students to think about the information they heard in the lecture. (You may want to play the audio again.)

- Give some examples of exam questions such as the following: *What are the three different types of plate boundaries?*

- You may want to discuss some different types of exam questions such as short-answer, multiple-choice, matching, and essay.

Exercise A.

- Make sure students write questions that can be answered from information presented in the text.

Exercise B.

- After students have answered each other's questions, write the questions on the board and take a vote on the best ones.

Exercise C. | Self-Reflection

- Explain that the first two questions give students an opportunity to reflect on the study strategies they have practiced in this unit.

- Be aware that question 3 may be a sensitive issue if students come from countries that have had devastating earthquakes.

45 mins

Exploring Spoken English
(pages 128-130)

Language Function: Using Transitions

- Go over the information in the box.

- Explain that the focus in this part of the lesson will be on transitions that show connections between sentences. Transitions are also important in academic writing.

- Explain what is meant by *train of thought* (sequence of ideas).

Exercise A.

- After reading the information in the chart, ask the following questions: Which type of transitions show that two pieces of information are different? (*contrast*) Which type shows similarities? (*addition*) Which type shows that one event happens because of another? (*result*) Which type introduces specific ideas? (*example*)

TIP Another way to use the chart in exercise A is to ask students to work in pairs. One student reads the sentences aloud in random order without the transitions. The other student identifies which transition is missing.

Exercise B.

- Allow time for students to write their answers.

- Ask volunteers to read their answers aloud. Note that there are two possible answers for each sentence.

Answer Key *(Answers may vary.)*

1. Therefore / As a result
2. However / On the other hand
3. For example / For instance
4. However / On the other hand
5. In addition / Furthermore

Grammar: Imperatives

- Ask students to describe the photo. Ask why this situation is potentially dangerous.

- Go over the information in the box.

IDEAS FOR... **Presenting Grammar**

- Ask what advice students would give to anyone who smells smoke in a movie theater.
- Make a list of students' ideas on the board.
- Point out the verbs that would be used in the imperative form for the advice.

Exercise A.

- Ask students what they know about how to prepare for an earthquake or what to do during an earthquake. Write their ideas on the board.

Answer Key *(Answers may vary.)*

keep, find, Have, Plan, Get (under), Stay (away), get (to), Help, call, Know, Listen to

Exercise B. | Collaboration

- Remind students to include negative imperatives in their sentences.

TIP In exercise B, you may want to assign one situation to each pair so that all topics are covered.

Exercise C. | Discussion

- Ask each pair of students to join another pair and share their ideas.

IDEAS FOR... **Expansion**

Ask students to work in groups. Each group should prepare a set of instructions for one of the situations below.

- To make friends at a new school or job
- To avoid getting lost when staying in a strange city
- To find a good place to live when you move to a new city

Students can read their instructions aloud or write them on posters.

Exercise D. | Role-Playing

- Have students look at the photo and describe what the children are doing.

- Go over the situation in the box.

- Allow time for students to complete the conversation together.

- Ask students to practice in pairs.

Exercise E.

- Put pairs together to make groups of four so that pairs perform their conversations for each other.

Exercise F. | Critical Thinking

- After discussing question 1, ask students to suggest other ways to prepare for an earthquake. For example, students may suggest that you prepare an emergency kit as well as buy flashlights and a battery-operated radio.

- For question 2, suggest that students look for clues in the conversation such as the phrases "Don't worry!" and "That's OK," where Student A is trying to reassure Student B.

Speaking *(page 131)*

30-45 mins

Giving a News Report

Exercise A.

- Ask students if they have ever wanted to be news reporters. What do they think is interesting or difficult about this job?

- Go over the situation in the box.

- Look at the photo at the bottom of the page and ask students to describe it.

Exercise B. | Planning a Presentation

- Make sure students understand the questions in the chart. For question 2, you may want to mention that earthquakes are usually measured on a Richter scale of 1–10. A strong earthquake causing major damage would be about 5. A minor earthquake causing little damage would be between 2 and 3.

- Explain that this news report is one that they will present orally, as if on the TV news. The information is fictional, but it should sound realistic.

Exercise C.

- Make sure students know they should each present part of the report, alternating turns as they present.

- Remind them to first introduce who they are and where they are. For example: *This is Kristy Donaldson reporting from San Francisco in California.*

Exercise D. | Presentation

- Have students practice in groups before presenting to the class.

- Ask the rest of the class to give feedback on each presentation. They could listen, for example, to whether the presenters included all the important information or left anything out.

- Optional: Ask for volunteers who would like to videotape their presentations. Play the recordings for the whole class and ask for feedback.

> **IDEAS FOR... Expansion**
>
> - Bring in a video news clip of a natural disaster (volcanic eruption, flood, wildfire, tornado, hurricane) from the TV news or the Internet. Have students take notes on the clip using a chart similar to the one in exercise **B**. Help them to identify useful phrases.
> - Bring in (or ask students to bring in) newspaper articles about a natural disaster. Have students use the information to prepare oral news reports based on the information.

Viewing: Volcano Trek

30 mins

(pages 132-133)

Overview of the Video | This video is about a research expedition to a volcano in Ethiopia.

Before Viewing

- Ask students to look at the pictures and say what they think the video will be about.

- Ask questions about the diagram and practice new vocabulary from the unit. For example: *What is at the top of a volcano? What comes out of it? What is underground? What is on the side?*

- Ask students to complete the information in the book. Check students' answers (see tip below).

> **TIP** One way to check the answers is to call out one of the words and have students respond with the corresponding number.

Answer Key	1. crater 2. magma 3. lava 4. lava lake 5. eruption

> **IDEAS FOR...** **Checking Comprehension**
>
> Ask students to write definitions of each of these new words in their vocabulary journals, draw a picture of it, and label it.

While Viewing

 Exercise A.
2:35
- Play the video while students circle the words from the previous exercise as they are mentioned.

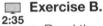 **Exercise B.**
2:35
- Read the statements aloud. Play the video again. Check the answers as a class.

> **TIP** Ask students to make the necessary change to turn the false sentences into true statements.

Answer Key	1. T 2. F 3. F 4. T 5. T 6. F

Exercise C. | Making Inferences
2:35
- Explain the meaning of *inference* (information that is not given specifically, but that we can deduce from other information that is given).

- Discuss the answer to the question as a class.

> **Answer Key** *(Answers may vary.)*
>
> It is likely that they enjoy their work because they are prepared to endure tough conditions to obtain their samples. They seem excited by what they are seeing.

After Viewing

Exercise A. | Self-Reflection

- Encourage students to write as many questions as they can.

Exercise B. | Discussion

- Have students share their answers in groups.

- Find out how many different questions the class was able to generate. Ask each group to share their best ideas with the class.

Exercise C. | Using a Graphic Organizer

- Look at the photo. Why is this job interesting? Why is it dangerous?

- Explain that students should write words or phrases in the chart (not full sentences).

- Draw the chart on the board and invite volunteers to come to the board to write their ideas.

Exercise D.

- Ask volunteers to read their sentences aloud. Remind them to use transitions.

Exercise E. | Critical Thinking

- After students have discussed these questions in pairs, discuss them as a class.

Pronunciation Note
Erta Ale: **ur**-ta ah-le

30 mins

Building and Using Vocabulary *(pages 134-135)*

WARM-UP

The Lesson B target vocabulary is presented in the context of information about people who live near volcanoes.

- Ask students why people are fascinated by volcanoes and what makes tourists want to visit them.

- Ask if they would like to visit a volcano and have them explain why or why not.

Building Vocabulary

Exercise A. | Prior Knowledge

- Discuss any volcanic eruptions that students have heard of. What were the effects of the eruptions? Has anyone in the class ever visited a volcano (active or dormant)?

- Discuss the questions as a class.

Exercise B. | Meaning from Context

track 2-20

- Have students look at the photo and guess what these people are doing and why.

- Point out the footnotes and go over them if your students need help with the new words.

- Play the audio while students read.

- Ask students to say what dangers of living near a volcano are mentioned in the text.

> **IDEAS FOR... Checking Comprehension**
>
> Divide the class into groups. Assign one paragraph to each group. Ask each group to prepare as many questions as they can about their paragraph. With books closed, students can choose a group to answer each question. To make this competitive, you can award points for each question asked and for each correct answer given.

Using Vocabulary

Exercise C.

- Set a time limit for students to complete the exercise.

Answer Key	**1.** d **2.** i **3.** j **4.** b **5.** g **6.** e **7.** f **8.** c **9.** h **10.** a

> **IDEAS FOR... Multi-level Classes**
>
> For some extra vocabulary practice, write sentences for each word on a separate card. Leave a blank for the target word. Write the target word on the back of the card. You can put words and corresponding sentences on different colored cards according to their difficulty. Ask students to select a card, hold it up so that their partner can see the answer, read the sentence, and guess the missing word.

Exercise D. | Critical Thinking

- Encourage students to evaluate and compare information from the video and the reading when answering this question.

- Ask students to find reasons to support both points of view.

Exercise E.

- Encourage students to think of creative and interesting ways to complete these sentences.

- For the more difficult words, students may want to record the sentences in their vocabulary journals.

Exercise F.

- Explain to students that paraphrasing the article in their own words will help them to remember the information and consolidate new vocabulary.

Pronunciation Note

Merapi: mur-**ah**-pee
Yogyakarta: yog-yuh-**kahr**-tuh
Krakatau: krak-uh-**tou**
Kinarejo: kin-er-**ah**-jo

Developing Listening Skills

(pages 136-137)

track 2-21

Pronunciation: Syllable Stress Review and Syllable Number

■ Go over the information in the box.

■ Remind students of the meaning of *syllable* and *syllable stress*, which were introduced on page 67.

track 2-22

Exercise A.

■ Ask students to say each word silently and predict the number of syllables.

■ Play the audio while students underline the syllables.

■ Check the answers as a class.

> **Answer Key** *(Answers may vary.)*
>
> 1. <u>ac</u> <u>cord</u> ing (to); three 2. <u>ac</u> tive; two 3. <u>af</u> fect; two
> 4. <u>di</u> sas ter; three 5. <u>e</u> rup tion; three 6. <u>e</u> vac u ate; four
> 7. <u>make</u> <u>a</u> <u>liv</u> ing; four 8. <u>na</u> tu ral; three 9. <u>vil</u> <u>la</u> ger; three

track 2-22

Exercise B.

■ Play the audio again as students circle the stressed syllable.

■ Ask students to repeat each word after the audio.

> **Answer Key** *(Answers may vary.)*
>
> 1. ac (cord) ing (to) 2. (ac) tive 3. af (fect) 4. di (sas) ter
> 5. e (rup) tion 6. e (vac) u ate 7. make a (liv) ing 8. (na) tu ral
> 9. (vil) la ger

Exercise C.

■ Do the first item as an example. Say either sentence *a* or sentence *b* and ask students to identify which one you said. Ask students to continue this exercise with a partner.

■ Discuss what the difference is between the pairs of sentences. Is it the number of syllables, the syllable stress, or a different phoneme?

> **TIP** To check that students have achieved the goal of this task, ask volunteers to read one sentence from each pair aloud. Have students raise their right hand for *a*, or their left hand for *b*.

Before Listening

Self-Reflection

■ When students have finished discussing their questions in pairs, draw a T-chart on the board and ask them to tell you their ideas. (See charts in the *Independent Student Handbook*, page 214.)

Listening: A Group Discussion

track 2-23

Exercise A. | Listening for Main Ideas

■ Go over the questions. Play the audio while students listen for the main ideas.

> **Answer Key** *(Answers may vary.)*
>
> 1. volcanoes and when to evacuate
> 2. to help each other prepare for an exam

track 2-23

Exercise B. | Listening for Details

■ Allow time for students to read the sentences.

■ Play the audio again.

> **Answer Key** *(Answers may vary.)*
>
> 1. inside 2. melted rock, lava 3. start fires 4. evacuate
> 5. 57 6. culture

> **IDEAS FOR...** **Checking Comprehension**
>
> Ask students to listen again and note the questions that these students ask. Pause the audio so that students can write them as a dictation. Highlight the grammar structures used to ask questions.
> 1. I don't understand the difference between lava and magma. Aren't they the same thing?
> 2. Who can explain why volcanoes are dangerous?
> 3. Did anyone understand the part about the man in Indonesia? Isn't it OK if he tells people when it's time to evacuate?

After Listening

Discussion | Use these questions to review and summarize the information presented so far in Lesson B.

45 mins

Exploring Spoken English
(pages 138-139)

Grammar: Gerunds as Subjects and Objects

- Explain that a gerund is the *-ing* form of a verb when it is used as a noun.

- Go over the information in the box.

- Ask students to suggest gerunds of their own to substitute for the ones used in the first two examples.

> **IDEAS FOR...   Presenting Grammar**
>
> Ask students to write down three things they are interested in, afraid of, and worried about. Then ask them to walk around the classroom and find out how many people are interested in, afraid of, and worried about the same things. Remind them to use gerunds in their sentences.

Exercise A.

- Invite volunteers to read their answers aloud.

- Ask them to identify which gerunds are subjects and which are objects.

Answer Key

1. Farming 2. being 3. Jogging 4. Having
5. losing 6. getting

Track 2-24

Exercise B. | Note-Taking

- Discuss the question with your students. Ask if the natural world is important to them. How?

- Play the audio while students take notes.

Answer Key

Hasan
Occupation: Soil scientist
Other notes: helps farmers care for land—farming, fishing important—heavy rain → flooding → rich soil

Margaret
Country: Switzerland
Other notes: Swiss cheese—mountains—moving cows = hard work

Cecilia
Occupation: High school student
Other notes: great weather so always outside—walking—time with friends—beach

Exercise C.

- Students can work in pairs to retell the information about each person. Remind them to use gerunds.

TIP   You may want to appoint one person in each group to make a note of each time a gerund is used.

Exercise D. | Remind students to take notes in words or phrases, not full sentences.

Exercise E. | Presentation

- Go over the information in the Presentation Skills box.

- Encourage students to speak clearly and slowly and pause from time to time while speaking (see below).

Presentation Skills: Speaking Slowly | You may want to demonstrate examples of someone speaking too quickly without pauses and someone speaking more slowly with pauses. You can do this by reading aloud the information in the box first very quickly and then more slowly. When you have finished, ask students which style they prefer and why.

Language Function: Refusing Politely

Discussion | Go over the information in the Student to Student box on polite refusals.

Student to Student: Polite Refusals

- Discuss whether these rules for polite refusals are the same in students' own culture.

- Note that in some cultures it is necessary to give very detailed excuses for refusing, but in English, just a brief sentence or two is usually enough.

Engage: Giving a Group Presentation *(page 140)*

45 mins

WARM-UP

Explain that students are going to work together in a group to prepare a group presentation about a natural disaster. Ask them to talk about any natural disasters that have been in the news recently. Remind students of presentation skills you have studied, such as using visuals and speaking slowly.

Exercise A. | Planning a Presentation

Briefly preview the whole process for students. First, go over the box at the top of the page. Point out that the presentation is about a type of disaster, not one specific drought, flood, etc. Announce the time limit for each presentation. Then go through the steps of the process:

1. Form a group.
2. Choose a topic.
3. Do research.
4. Organize information.
5. Create a visual.
6. Plan and practice presentation.
7. Give a presentation in class.

- Explain the meaning of any unknown words (refer to photos on this page).

- Put students into groups of three or four.

- Make sure that a variety of topics is chosen. If possible, ask each group to choose a different type of disaster.

Exercise B.

- If possible, have students research their topic on the Internet or take the class to a library to find more information.

> **TIP** Presentations based on research are more interesting and authentic than those that include only general knowledge.

Exercise C.

- Help students to complete the outline with appropriate information.

Exercise D.

- Help students to decide what kind of visual will best support their presentations.

- Suggest that students can also download pictures or diagrams from the Internet, if available. Designing the visual could be the responsibility of one member or pair of students, or the whole group could work on the task together.

Exercise E.

- Remind students that every member of the group should present a part of the presentation. One member should also introduce the topic and explain what the presentation will be about.

- Allow time for students to practice in groups before exercise **F**.

Exercise F. | Presentation

- Remind students of the time limit for each presentation.

- Discuss the relevant criteria for assessing presentations. Tell students you will be asking the following questions as you watch their presentations: Do they speak clearly? Do they look at the audience? Do they speak slowly and pause from time to time? Do they use clear visuals? Do they use language for talking about visuals, as taught on page 120? Is the presentation informative and interesting? Is the information well organized?

- Your evaluation chart may look similar to this one:

Presentation Evaluation Chart					
Speaks slowly and clearly	1	2	3	4	5
Makes eye contact	1	2	3	4	5
Use of visuals	1	2	3	4	5
Well organized	1	2	3	4	5
Interesting content	1	2	3	4	5

> **TIP** You may want to develop a peer evaluation sheet for students to use when listening to each other's presentations. This could be passed out or put on the board at the preview stage.

IDEAS FOR... Expansion

Ask students to put a summary of their presentation on the classroom wall or on the class Web site.

Ancient Peoples and Places

Academic Track
**Anthropology and
Sociology/Archaeology**

Academic Pathways:
Lesson A: Listening to a Guided Tour
Presenting an Ancient Artifact
Lesson B: Listening to a Conversation
between Students
Giving a Summary

Unit Theme

This unit explores some interesting facts about ancient historical sites around the world.

Unit 8 explores the topic of ancient civilizations as it relates to:
– an ancient royal tomb in Guatemala
– Mayan pyramids
– the seven wonders of the ancient world

– the city of Machu Picchu
– the Egyptian pharaoh Tutankhamen
– an ancient palace in Hanoi

Think and Discuss *(page 141)*

5 mins

- Ask students to describe the photo.

- Discuss the questions. Some students may know the answers. If they don't, have them make an educated guess.

Answer Key

1. the Mayans

2. It was a temple and a royal tomb.

3. (*Answers may vary.*) several civilizations in present-day Mexico, Guatemala, Peru, Egypt, and Sudan

Exploring the Theme: Ancient Peoples and Places

15 mins

(pages 142-143)

Exercise A.

The opening spread features a world map and pictures of several ancient civilizations.

- Ask students to look at the pictures and read the captions.

- Ask questions to check comprehension. (See box for suggestions.)

- Discuss questions 1 and 2. Look at the map key and read the information.

Exercise B.

- Discuss questions 1–3. Discuss which of these cultures students know something about and which ones are new to them.

Answer Key

1. Mayan Civilization, Inca Empire, Ancient Egypt

2. Ecuador, Peru, Bolivia, Argentina, Chile, Colombia

3. Great Zimbabwe and Ancient Egypt; Mayan Civilization

4. (*Answers will vary.*)

IDEAS FOR...   **Checking Comprehension**

After students have looked at the pictures and read the captions, ask questions to check their comprehension. For example:
Which civilization was ruled by pharaohs?
(*the Egyptians*)
Which city was built in the 3rd century BC?
(*Mohenjo Daro*)
Which civilization was located in Vietnam?
(*Thang Long*)
Which civilization ended in the 15th century?
(*Great Zimbabwe*)

Pronunciation Note
Pachacuti: pa-cha-**koo**-tee
Thang: Tah-ng

Building and Using Vocabulary *(pages 144-145)*

30 mins

WARM-UP

The Lesson A target vocabulary is presented in the context of an archaeological discovery.

- Ask students to explain the terms *archaeology* and *archaeologist*. Suggest that students try to come up with their own definitions first and then compare their definitions to the ones found in a dictionary.

- Ask students whether they think archaeology is important. What can we learn from ancient historical sites? Why are scientists and historians interested in them?

Building Vocabulary

track 3-2

Exercise A. | Meaning from Context

- Have students look at the pictures and describe them.

- Have students look at the map and ask them to describe San Bartolo's exact location.

- Ask students what topic they think the photos and captions relate to.

- Play the audio while students read.

Exercise B.

- Encourage students to use the context to work out the meanings of the words in blue. Practice the pronunciation of new words if needed. For example, *tomb* (silent *b*), *ancient, mural,* and *buried* might cause some difficulty.

Answer Key

1. tomb	**5.** mural	**9.** reveal
2. images	**6.** royal	**10.** pyramid
3. dig	**7.** ancient	
4. buried	**8.** site	

Using Vocabulary

Exercise A.

- Allow time for students to read the text and write their answers.

- Encourage students to try to remember the words before looking back at page 144.

Answer Key

1. site	**5.** tomb	**9.** revealed
2. ancient	**6.** royal	**10.** images
3. pyramid	**7.** buried	
4. mural	**8.** dig	

Exercise B.

- Encourage students to use the new vocabulary in their discussion.

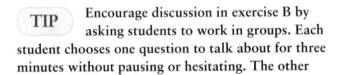

TIP Encourage discussion in exercise B by asking students to work in groups. Each student chooses one question to talk about for three minutes without pausing or hesitating. The other students give points for his or her performance.

Exercise C. | Discussion

- Suggest that students write three or four facts about ancient civilizations in their own country and see if the other members of the class agree with them if they are from the same country. (People can often have very different ideas about historical "facts.")

- Ask students if they would like to visit the site in the photo. Why, or why not?

Developing Listening Skills
(pages 146-147)

45 mins

Pronunciation: Question Intonation

- Remind students of the difference in intonation between *yes/no* questions and *wh-* questions.

- Give some examples of *yes/no* questions and *wh-* questions. Ask students to determine if the intonation rises or falls.

- Read the information and the examples in the box.

 Exercises A and B.

track 3-3

- Play the audio.

- Play the audio again and pause while students repeat each example.

Exercise C.

- Suggest that students write questions connected to the theme of the lesson (e.g., *Why do people study ancient sites?*).

Before Listening

Prior Knowledge

- Have students work with a partner to ask and answer the questions.

- Remind them to use correct question intonation.

- Invite volunteers to ask and answer questions for the whole class.

Listening: A Guided Tour

 Exercise A. | Listening for Main Ideas

track 3-4

- Ask volunteers to read the questions aloud.

- Play the audio while students circle the answers.

- Go over the answers as a class.

Answer Key   1. c 2. a 3. a

 Exercise B. | Listening for Details

track 3-4

- Read the questions aloud.

- Play the audio while students take notes.

Answer Key

1. the Late Classic period / AD 600–900

2. an old story

3. five

4. the ball court

5. the Jaguar Throne

6. a wild cat

IDEAS FOR...   Checking Comprehension

Ask these additional questions or write them on the board.

1. When was the Late Classic period? (*AD 600–900*)
2. How long is the tour? (*90 minutes*)
3. What was the Mayan name for this pyramid? (*It is not known.*)
4. How long did it take to build? (*hundreds of years*)
5. What does the Jaguar Throne look like? (*It looks like a jaguar with two heads. In the animal's middle is a kind of seat.*)

After Listening

Collaboration

- Brainstorm a few questions with the class.

- Allow time for students to write their ideas.

- Ask each pair to write their most interesting question on the board.

- Ask the class to vote on the best questions.

IDEAS FOR...   Multi-level Classes

Challenge higher-level students to choose one of their questions and research the answer for homework. They can present the information in the next class. An easier option would be for students to find three interesting facts about the Mayan civilization and present them to the class at the next meeting.

Exploring Spoken English

(pages 148-150)

45 mins

Grammar: The Passive Voice with the Past

Exercise A. | Prior Knowledge

- Remind students that the passive voice in the present tense was presented in Unit 4, page 69. As well as introducing the past form of the passive voice, this grammar box also provides information about the omission of the agent when it is unknown or unimportant.

- Ask students to compare the form and the meaning of the two sentences.

- Help students to identify the subject and verb of each sentence. (*They / buried; The king / was buried*)

- Have students tell you who *they* refers to in the first sentence.

- Go over the information in the box.

- Ask students to make up additional examples. (See box below for suggestions.)

> **IDEAS FOR... Presenting Grammar**
>
> Ask students to make up some sentences with the passive voice using information about the Egyptian pyramids. For example:
>
> The pyramids were built by the ancient Egyptians.
> A pharaoh was buried with many of his possessions.
> Their tombs were discovered many years later.

Exercise B.

- Allow time for students to write their answers.

- Ask volunteers to read their answers aloud.

Answer Key

1. was built 2. were planted 3. was constructed
4. was destroyed 5. was kept 6. were carried
7. was designed

Exercise C. | Discussion

- Ask students to discuss what these places have in common and why they think these sites were chosen as the seven wonders of the ancient world.

Exercise D.

track 3-5

- Have students look at the photos and ask them what they know about each of these places.

- Ask students to look at the title and predict what the text will be about.

- Play the audio while students listen and underline uses of the passive.

- Ask students to tell you which passive voice verbs are followed by a phrase using *by*.

Answer Key

Students should underline the following uses of the passive voice: were chosen (by one person), were encouraged (by their government), were nominated, were registered, were announced, were announced

Exercise E. | Critical Thinking

- Encourage students to think about the information in the text. Was the project useful or interesting? Was the method used appropriate? Why, or why not? Students may have different opinions. Encourage them to support their opinions.

Exercise F. | Discussion

- Before looking at the chart on page 150, you may want students to try and guess which places they think will appear on the list.

Pronunciation Note

Nebuchadnezzar: neb-uh-kuhd-**nez**-er

Language Function: Using the Passive Voice to Talk about Famous Sites

- Read the information and the examples in the box.

- Mention that an alternative, more informal, form of the second question is also possible: *Who was it built by?*

- Have students practice *wh-* questions with the passive voice using *what, why, where, who*, and *how* by asking about the Egyptian pyramids, or about any of the original seven wonders of the world mentioned on page 148.

Exercise A. | Discussion

- Allow time for students to read the information about the new seven wonders of the world.

- Ask a few comprehension questions: *Where is Petra? Who was the Taj Mahal built by?*

- Have students refer back to the photos on page 149.

- Ask students if they know any additional information about any of these places.

Exercise B. | Remind students to use the passive voice as much as possible.

Exercise C.

- Tell students that no question may be used more than once.

- Ask several students what question they found the most difficult.

IDEAS FOR... Expansion

Have students make up a general knowledge quiz using questions in the passive voice. They should ask about other famous historical buildings or sites in their country or around the world. Check their questions for accuracy while they are writing. Then invite students to ask the class their questions and find out who knows the answer. For example: How was Pompeii destroyed? Who were the Pyramids of Giza built by? (By whom were the Pyramids of Giza built?)

Speaking *(page 151)*

30-45 mins

Presenting an Ancient Artifact

Exercise A.

- Ask students to cover the captions and try to guess what these artifacts were used for and who they were made by.

- Tell students to uncover the captions. Go over them as a class.

- For each artifact, have students raise their hands if their guesses were accurate.

Exercise B. | At the end of the discussion, ask the class as a whole which artifact they found most interesting and why.

> **TIP** Remind students to make sure everyone in the group has a turn asking the questions. If you do not have even groups of three in your class, have one or two groups of four and allow two students to share one object.

Exercise C. | Planning a Presentation

- If you are planning to evaluate the presentations, tell students that you will give extra points for imaginative content.

Exercise D. | Remind students to introduce the topic of each segment of their presentation. For example: A: *I am going to talk about an Anasazi artifact.*

Exercise E. | Presentation Remind students to speak clearly and slowly with frequent pauses during their presentations.

> **TIP** An alternative way to handle this presentation is to give one artifact to each group and have each person present the answer to just one of the questions in exercise B.

> **TIP** Suggest some ways that students can ask their peers for feedback on their presentations. For example: *Did we talk slowly enough? Were our ideas well organized?*

Viewing: The Lost City of Machu Picchu *(pages 152-153)*

30 mins

Overview of the Video | This video is about the ancient historical site of Machu Picchu in Peru and how it is being affected by tourism.

Before Viewing

Exercise A. | Discussion

■ Ask students to look at the photo and think of some words to describe this place.

■ Ask students to look at the map and describe Machu Picchu's exact location.

Exercise B.

■ Ask students to suggest definitions for the words in the box. Then have them use a dictionary to compare their definitions to the ones in the dictionary.

 track 3-6

Exercise C.

■ Ask students to read the text and fill in the blanks.

■ Play the audio as students check their answers.

Answer Key	1. mountains 2. civilization 3. explorer 4. damage 5. tourism

While Viewing

 2:31

Exercise A.

■ Play the video while students take notes. Point out that two places are shown in the video.

■ Encourage students to use the passive voice (past or present) in their discussions.

■ Write a few verbs on the board to help students make complete sentences: *build, call, find, visit, make, sell.*

 2:31

Exercise B.

■ Read the statements aloud.

■ Play the video again.

■ Go over the answers.

■ Ask students to make changes to the false sentences to turn them into true statements.

Answer Key	1. F 2. T 3. T 4. T

Critical Thinking Focus: Making Inferences

■ Go over the information in the box.

■ Give an example of an inference. For example, the video says, *For a long time [Machu Picchu] was lost to the outside world.* From the phrase *the outside world*, we can infer that local people knew of Machu Picchu, but Americans and Europeans did not.

Exercise C. | Making Inferences

2:31

■ Read the quotations and play the video or section of the video again.

■ Ask students what Jose's business is.

■ This exercise can be done individually or as a class discussion.

■ Ask students what they think conservationists are worried about. How could tourism damage Machu Picchu and its natural environment?

After Viewing

Exercise A. | Collaboration

■ Have students share their questions with the class.

■ Optional: Assign one question to each pair to research for homework.

Exercise B. | Discussion

■ These questions help students review the information in the unit thus far as well as prepare for Lesson B.

Building and Using Vocabulary *(pages 154-155)*

WARM-UP

The Lesson B target vocabulary is presented in the context of excavating ancient sites.

- Ask students to discuss how they think modern technological advances have improved our ability to excavate and learn about ancient sites.

Building Vocabulary

track 3-7

Exercise A. | Meaning from Context

- Discuss the photos and ask what students already know about Tutankhamen.

- Play the audio while students read the text.

- Ask which information in the text students found most surprising or interesting.

Exercise B.

- Explain that when you see an unfamiliar word, working out what type of word it is can help you to work out its meaning.

- Draw the chart on the board and ask three volunteers to come to the board. Have the other students tell them what to write in each column.

- Ask students which verb in the text is in the passive voice. *(was murdered)*

Answer Key

Noun	Verb	Adjective
treasures	reported	precious
race	rules	alive
	murdered	
	analyze	
	solve	
	determine	

IDEAS FOR...   Checking Comprehension

After listening and reading the text, ask students to close their books and tell you as much as they can remember about it. Then ask them to open their books and check if they were right.

Using Vocabulary

Exercise C.

- Encourage students to try to remember the words before looking back at the text.

Answer Key

1. treasures	5. reported	9. race
2. analyze	6. murdered	10. determine
3. precious	7. ruled	
4. solve	8. alive	

Exercise D.

- Encourage students to write their own sentences using these words and record them in their vocabulary journals.

Answer Key

1. analyzes 2. treasures 3. ruled 4. report 5. races

Exercise E. | Discussion

- Encourage students to think of other questions using these new words. You could make this into a competition and award points for the highest number of correct questions.

IDEAS FOR...   Expansion

- Ask students to think of questions they would like to ask about Tutankhamen and assign one question for each pair to research for homework.

- Ask students to discuss the importance of museums and why they are useful. Ask students for their opinions about whether ancient treasures should always be kept in their country of origin, or if they should be allowed to go to other countries.

Pronunciation Note

Tutankhamen: toot-ahng-**kah**-muhn
Akhenaten: ahkna-**tin**

Developing Listening Skills

45 mins

(pages 156-157)

Before Listening

Exercise A.

- Ask a few general comprehension questions; *What was the documentary about? What was discovered? How it was it discovered?*

- Help students to identify abbreviations in the notes—*diff (different), c (century), gov't (government)*—and use of numerals *1000's (thousands)*. Ask students to suggest any other words in the notes that could be abbreviated.

Exercise B.

- Tell students to work in pairs and take turns talking about Silvio's notes.

- Ask students to rewrite the notes using complete sentences.

- Call on volunteers to read one of their complete sentences to the class. Ask the rest of the class if it is correct.

Listening: A Conversation between Students

track 3-8

Exercise A. | Listening for Main Ideas

- Read the questions aloud.

- Play the audio while students take notes.

- Go over the answers as a class.

> **Answer Key**
>
> **1.** communication class **2.** give an oral summary of a movie or TV program **3.** He doesn't know how to summarize.

track 3-8

Exercise B. | Listening for Details

- Allow time for students to read the sentences and answer choices.

- Play the audio again while students choose their answers.

- Go over the answers as a class.

> **Answer Key**   **1.** c **2.** b **3.** b

track 3-8

Exercise C. | Making Inferences

- Remind students that the correct answers are not stated explicitly. Their answers will be based on inference.

- Play the audio again.

- Ask students' opinion of the *wh-* questions technique for summarizing that Laura describes. Do they already do this? Do they think it would be helpful?

> **Answer Key**   **1.** F **2.** T **3.** T **4.** F

> **IDEAS FOR...**   **Checking Comprehension**
>
> Ask students to summarize the technique that Laura recommends. For example:
>
> The technique is called the "*wh-* questions technique for summarizing." You ask yourself *who, what, when, where, why,* and *how.* For instance, who was involved in the story you watched?

After Listening

Exercise A. | Planning a Presentation   Use these questions to review and summarize the information from this lesson.

> **Answer Key**
>
> The people involved were construction workers, archaeologists, and the government. The site was discovered in 2002. It was discovered during the construction of a new building. It is important because it is the site of an ancient royal palace.

Exercise B. | Presentation

- Give feedback on whether students covered all the main points in their summaries.

> **IDEAS FOR...**   **Expansion**
>
> Ask students to use *wh-* questions to summarize another text from this unit (page 145, 149, 152, or 154).

Exploring Spoken English
(pages 158-159)

30 mins

Grammar: Phrasal Verbs

- Go over the information in the box.

- Demonstrate the literal and nonliteral meaning of *look up* by miming the actions of looking up (at the sky) and looking up a word in a dictionary.

> **IDEAS FOR...** Presenting Grammar
>
> Give some other examples of phrasal verbs that have two meanings (literal and nonliteral). For example:
>
> He **took off** his coat. (= remove)
> The plane **took off**. (= departed)
>
> I **turned down** the music. (= reduced volume)
> I **turned down** the job. (= refused)

Exercise A.

- Invite volunteers to read their answers aloud.

- Ask them to suggest synonyms for the phrasal verbs in the box. Some examples include *hand in* = give to the teacher; *leave out* = omit, not include; *pay back* = return; *get together* = meet; *close down* = close completely; *help out* = assist, give a hand.

Answer Key

1. pay, back 2. close down 3. leave out 4. get together
5. hand, in 6. help out

Language Function: Discussing Problems

Student to Student: Voicing a Small Problem

- Read the information in the box.

- Ask students to suggest ways to finish these sentences and practice saying them with appropriate intonation.

Exercise A.

- Allow time for students to practice in pairs and then switch roles and practice again.

- Recognize students' use of appropriate intonation.

- Invite volunteers to read the conversation aloud to the class.

- Ask students to identify the phrasal verbs.

Exercise B. | Role-Playing

- Ask students to work in pairs.

- Remind students that the purpose is to practice the language for voicing a small problem.

- Ask two or three pairs to present their conversation to the class.

> **IDEAS FOR...** Expansion
>
> Give out some problems on index cards and have students practice the target phrases. Example problems could include:
> - You lost your friend's book.
> - You can't go to a friend's birthday party.
> - Your friend wants to borrow your laptop, but you need it.

Exercise C. | Discussion

- Discuss any different feelings or opinions students may have about talking about problems. In their countries or among their friends, is it usual to come straight to the point? Or is it more polite to approach the matter more indirectly?

Engage: Giving a Summary Presentation *(page 160)*

45 mins

WARM-UP

Have students name famous ancient historical sites around the world. If possible, bring in some pictures and have students share any information they know about the places. Ask them to talk about any ancient historical sites they have visited and say what was interesting about them. List them on the board.

Exercise A. | Preview the steps of this activity:

1. Choose a topic.
2. Do research and take notes.
3. Select main ideas from notes.
4. Select details for 2–3 main ideas.
5. Plan presentation.
6. Practice presentation.
7. Give presentation.

- Discuss the topics in general and help each student to choose one.

- Students may also choose from the list of ancient sites that they generated in the warm-up.

Presentation Skills: Oral Summaries

- Go over the information in the box.

- Explain that this presentation is a summary of facts based on research, not a summary of an argument, theory, or opinion.

Exercise B. | Using a Graphic Organizer

- Encourage students to research their topics independently on the Internet, or take the class to a library to find information.

- Remind students to write notes in the chart, not full sentences.

TIP Another way to handle this activity—especially if student access to research resources is limited—is to provide information about each of these places. Organize students into groups and give one set of information to each group. For the presentation stage, re-organize the groups so that one member from each group is represented in a new group. Then each student in the new group can present information about a different place.

Exercise C. | Planning a Presentation

- Set a time limit for each presentation.

- Remind students to introduce the topic and pause between each main point.

- Point out that students can choose the best order of questions that will be most logical for their topic.

- Discuss the criteria for assessing presentations or hand out copies of the evaluation chart. In this chart, 1 is the lowest score and 5 is the highest score.

Presentation Evaluation Chart					
Speaks slowly and clearly	1	2	3	4	5
Includes all main points	1	2	3	4	5
Includes interesting details	1	2	3	4	5
Well organized	1	2	3	4	5

Exercise D. | Presentation If possible, have students audio- or videotape their presentations. Encourage them to watch and/or listen to their presentation and look for ways to improve it. They can use the evaluation chart to do this.

IDEAS FOR... Expansion

- For homework, ask students to research more information about one aspect of their chosen topic (who, what, where, when, how, or why). They can bring in photos, diagrams, or other visuals to support their presentation.

- For homework, ask students to prepare a written version of their oral summary.

Species Survival

Academic Track
Life Science

Academic Pathways:

Lesson A: Listening to a Biologist's Talk
about Birds
Discussing Endangered Species

Lesson B: Listening to a Conversation about
a Science Experiment
Planning and Presenting a
Research Proposal

Unit Theme

This unit explores some interesting facts about animal and bird species.

Unit 9 explores the topic of how animal species survive as it relates to:
– Darwin's voyage around South America and
his theory of natural selection
– the African origin of humans
– specialized traits of birds

– endangered species
– a scientific expedition to the Congo Basin
– classifying species

Think and Discuss *(page 161)*

5 mins

- Ask students what they know about giraffes. Have they ever seen one? Where did they see it?

- Discuss the two questions.

- Mention some interesting facts about giraffes: *The average lifespan of a giraffe is 25 years in the wild and more than 30 years in captivity. Giraffes sleep for between 20 minutes and two hours a day. Giraffes are vegetarians. They use their tongues to pull leaves off trees. They are the tallest animals on earth.*

Exploring the Theme: Species Survival *(pages 162-163)*

15 mins

The opening spread features a photo of the Galápagos Islands and some information about Charles Darwin and his theory of natural selection, or the evolution of species.

- Discuss the questions as a class.

- Tell students to look at the map and describe the exact location of the islands.

- Tell students to look at the photos and read the information.

- Discuss why some species are endangered and what can be done to prevent their extinction.

- Make a list of animal species that students know of that are endangered.

IDEAS FOR... Expansion

Ask students to research the Galápagos Islands and find information about their history, their wildlife, and their connection to Charles Darwin. Have students share their information with a partner or in small groups.

Building and Using Vocabulary *(pages 164-165)*

30 mins

WARM-UP

The Lesson A target vocabulary is presented in the context of information about Charles Darwin and the development of his ideas about natural selection.

- Ask students what they think the scientific goals of this voyage may have been.

- Discuss what traveling by sea was like in the 1800s and how mapmaking and navigation have changed.

Building Vocabulary

track 3-9

Exercise A. | Meaning from Context

- Look at the map and ask students to describe the route of the *Beagle*. (On the voyage out, Darwin stopped at the Canary Islands just off the coast of Africa and then sailed on to Brazil and around South America. On the voyage home, sailing from the east, the *Beagle* touched Brazil again and then headed back to England.)

- Play the audio while students read.

- Ask questions to check comprehension. (See box below for suggestions.)

- Note: *H.M.S.* means *His (or Her) Majesty's Ship*.

> **IDEAS FOR...   Checking Comprehension**
>
> Ask questions to check comprehension.
> 1. What was the official purpose of the *Beagle's* voyage?
> 2. What did Darwin find interesting about the *rhea* in Argentina?
> 3. What was Darwin trying to explain?
> 4. Why did he think some species had developed and changed over time?

Exercise B.

- Encourage students to use the context to work out the meanings of the words in blue.

- Practice the pronunciation of syllable stress in new words such as *environment*, *diversity*, *identify*, *reproduce*, and *inherit*.

Answer Key

1. environment	**5.** traits	**9.** process
2. identify	**6.** reproduce	**10.** inherit
3. offspring	**7.** adapt	
4. diversity	**8.** species	

Using Vocabulary

Exercise A.

- Ask students to look at the map and think about what it shows.

- Point out the migration dates.

- Allow time for students to read the text and complete their answers.

- Go over the answers with the whole class.

- Go over the map again. Have students describe the routes from Africa to Australia; from Africa to Europe; and from Africa to Asia, North America, and South America. Ask which route took the shortest time? Which route took the longest time?

- Ask students to summarize the text in their own words.

Answer Key

diversity, reproduced, inherited, traits, process

Exercise B. | Discussion

- Encourage students to use the new vocabulary in their discussion.

- Advise students to record new vocabulary in their journals with their own example sentences.

Developing Listening Skills

45 mins

(pages 166-167)

Before Listening

Taking Brief Notes

Strategy #1: Write Only Key Words

- Discuss some of the difficulties with taking notes from lectures. Brainstorm tips and advice on how to take notes in lectures.

- Explain that students will study two strategies for note-taking in this lesson. Go over the information in the box.

 track 3-10

Exercises A and B. | Note-Taking

- Play the audio while students take notes. Check answers by asking students to call out their words as you write them on the board.

> **TIP** Emphasize that there are many possible ways of abbreviating and students should choose the ones that work best for them.

Strategy #2: Use Abbreviations

- Go over the information in the box. Brainstorm some other examples of abbreviations that are useful for note-taking including the following: = (is the same as), ≠ (is not the same as), @ (at), etc.

 track 3-10

Exercise C. | Note-Taking

- Ask students to start a new page in their notebooks to take new notes, this time using abbreviations. Play the audio again.

Exercise D.

- Invite two or three volunteers to write their answers on the board so that the class can compare different ways of taking notes.

Listening: A Biologist's Talk about Birds

Exercise A. | Predicting Content

- Brainstorm ideas with the class and write them on the board. Ask students to suggest vocabulary related to birds that the biologist may use.

Critical Thinking Focus: Using a Graphic Organizer to Take Notes | Make sure that students understand the two ways of using a graphic organizer. We can use one to take notes during a lecture (if we know in advance what kind of information we are going to hear), and we can use one to rewrite our notes after a lecture in a more systematic way so that our notes are easier to review.

 track 3-11

Exercise B. | Using a Graphic Organizer

- Go over the chart with students and discuss what information is missing. Play the audio while students complete the chart.

Answer Key *(Answers may vary.)*	
	greenfinch
UK, parts of Europe	
Male: long beak Female: shorter beak	large, strong beak
	M & F: large seeds
Fall & winter in warmer parts of Europe	

 track 3-11

Exercise C. | Critical Thinking

- Have students compare notes. Play the audio again if necessary.

> **IDEAS FOR...** **Checking Comprehension**
>
> Ask students to rewrite the information in their notes as complete sentences that describe the features of the goldfinch and the greenfinch.

After Listening

Exercise A. | Collaboration

- Assign this task for homework so students can research information about their topic before the presentation.

Exercise B. | Presentation

- Set a time limit for the presentations and suggest that each group ask at least three questions after each one. Invite volunteers to present their species to the class.

45
mins

Exploring Spoken English
(pages 168-170)

Pronunciation: Full and Reduced Vowel Sounds and Secondary Stress

track 3-12
Exercise A.

- Quickly review the concepts of syllables and stressed syllables.

- Play the audio or read the words aloud. Have students answer the questions together as a class after hearing each word.

Answer Key

banana:	**1.** three	**2.** 2nd	**3.** three
demand:	**1.** two	**2.** 2nd	**3.** two
answer:	**1.** two	**2.** 1st	**3.** two

track 3-13
- Explain that schwa is a word used to describe a reduced vowel sound.

- Play the audio. Help students hear the stressed and unstressed syllables by clapping the stress pattern. For example, *banana* would be *clap CLAP clap*.

- Note: You may want to wait until exercise **C** before reading the information about secondary stress.

IDEAS FOR... **Practicing Pronunciation**

Give each student an index card with a word on it that has three or four syllables. Have them walk around the classroom saying their word. Have them find other students with words that have the same number of syllables and stress pattern.

---

track 3-14
Exercise B.

- Play the audio while students underline the main stressed syllable in each word.

- Play the audio and have students repeat each word. (Clap your hands for each syllable as before.)

Answer Key

1. <u>prac</u> ti cal **2.** at <u>tach</u> ment **3.** pro <u>por</u> tion **4.** com <u>pare</u> **5.** a <u>vail</u> a ble **6.** sup <u>port</u>

track 3-15
Exercise C.

- Read the information about secondary stress in the box.

- Play the audio while students underline syllables with main stress and circle those with secondary stress.

- Review the difference between unstressed syllables with a reduced vowel sound, stressed syllables with a full vowel sound, and secondary stress syllables with a full vowel sound.

Answer Key

1. (re) com mend **4.** clas si (fy)
2. at mos (phere) **5.** quan ti (ty)
3. (ro) man tic **6.** (dis) ap pear

Exercise D.

- Write one or two names of famous people on the board and ask students to identify the syllables and the stress patterns of the names.

- Suggest that students record syllable stress of new words in their vocabulary notebooks.

Grammar: The Simple Present with Facts

- Explain that one important use of the simple present is for facts—statements that are usually or generally true.

Exercises A and B.

- Ask students to turn the false statements into true statements by using their general knowledge. Point out the answers at the bottom of the page.

Answer Key

1. live, F (Penguins live in Antarctica.) **2.** sleeps, T **3.** have, F (Bears have 42 teeth.) **4.** weighs, T **5.** use, T

IDEAS FOR... **Presenting Grammar**

Ask students to make up more sentences about animals, some true and some false. All sentences should use the present tense. Then ask volunteers to write their sentences on the board with blanks for the verbs. Have the other students guess the missing words.

Language Function: Explaining Causes and Effects

- Go over the information and examples in the box. Explain the difference between these two types of linking words. *Because* and *since* are used to show the relationship between two clauses in the same sentence. *As a result* and *therefore* are used to show a relationship between two sentences.

- Point out the punctuation used with *because* and *since*. When the result clause (beginning with *because* or *since*) comes first, it is followed by a comma. When the result clause is second, the comma is not needed.

- Point out the punctuation with *as a result* and *therefore*. They come at the beginning of a sentence and are followed by a comma.

Exercise A.

- Read the sentences aloud. Play the audio while students write down the signal words and phrases they hear.

- Make sure students know that they can write the words on the side of the page or in their notebooks. (They don't have to connect them to specific sentences yet.)

Answer Key	1. because 2. therefore 3. as a result

TIP If you think this exercise is difficult for your students, you can tell them they will hear three different cause-and-effect words or phrases.

Exercise B.

- Use the example in the speech bubble to introduce the exercise.

- Remind students to use any of the signal words in the box.

- Invite volunteers to read their sentences to the class. Discuss alternative answers.

Speaking *(page 171)*

30-45 mins

Discussing Endangered Species

Exercise A. | Prior Knowledge

- Look at the photo and read the questions.

- For question 1, brainstorm a list of animals that students think are endangered and write them on the board. For question 2, write a list of possible reasons on the board. Invite a volunteer from the class to lead a class discussion for question 3.

Exercise B. | Allow time for students to read about the Iberian lynx. Ask some comprehension questions: *Why has the lynx population decreased? How many are left?*

Exercise C. | Brainstorming

- After students have finished working in pairs, invite volunteers to come to the board and write their ideas in a chart.

Presentation Skills: Choosing Information to Support Your Topic | Explain that brainstorming and using a T-chart are ways of generating and organizing ideas that students may decide to use in the debate in exercise **D**.

Exercise D.

- Explain that a debate is different from a discussion. In a debate, one side presents an argument. Then the other side presents their opposing argument. At the end, listeners decide whose arguments are more convincing.

- Remind students to use phrases for explaining cause and effect in their debate.

IDEAS FOR... **Multi-level Classes**

Ask students to choose the activity they would like to do for homework.

- Research another endangered species and present the information to the class.

- Write their arguments for homework in the form of an essay.

Viewing: A Disappearing World *(pages 172-173)*

30 mins

Overview of the Video | This video is about a team of scientists who travel to the Congo Basin in central Africa to inventory the wildlife there.

Before Viewing

Exercise A. | Using a Dictionary

- Ask students to look at the photos and describe the vegetation and the landscape.

- Ask students to look at the map and describe the location of the Congo Basin.

- Ask students if they can define any of the words before looking at the definitions.

Answer Key   1. c 2. f 3. a 4. e 5. d 6. g 7. b

TIP   **If some students finish early, ask them to move around the classroom and help other students.**

Exercise B. | Prior Knowledge

- Find out if students know why some animal species have become endangered, such as polar bears (*global warming*), whales and elephants (*hunting*), and pandas (*loss of habitat due to human population*).

- Have students take the quiz and discuss the answers.

Exercise C. | Predicting Content

- Ask students what they know about the Congo Basin, especially about the wildlife and the terrain.

While Viewing

Exercise A.

3:17

- Allow time for students to read the sentences.

- Remind students that all the answers will be numbers.

- Play the video while students write their answers.

- Check the answers by asking students to dictate the answers to you as you write them on the board.

Answer Key   **1.** one quarter **2.** half **3.** eight **4.** 70, 80 **5.** 360 **6.** 15

Exercise B. | Note-Taking

3:17

- Review strategies for note-taking from this unit (using key words and abbreviations).

- Play the video again.

Exercise C.

- After working in pairs, ask students to share their ideas with the class.

- As a follow-up activity, play the video again so students can check how much they retold correctly.

Answer Key *(Answers may vary.)*

- contains almost 1/4 world's rain forests

- may have up to 1/2 wild plants & animals in Africa

- may disappear soon

IDEAS FOR...   Expansion

Play the video with the sound turned off and ask students to supply the narration in their own words.

After Viewing

Critical Thinking

- Before forming groups, go over the three questions with the class.

- Ask volunteers to describe the bird-watching trip from page 167 mentioned in question 2.

- As a follow-up, ask what else could help save the Congo Basin.

TIP   **If necessary, review the bird-watching trip from page 167 so that everyone can answer question 2.**

IDEAS FOR...   Multi-level Classes

Challenge higher-level students by asking them to find out about other scientific studies of animals, for example, Dian Fossey's work with mountain gorillas in the rainforests of Rwanda and the Congo. They can present their information in a later class.

Building and Using Vocabulary *(pages 174-175)*

30 mins

WARM-UP

The Lesson B target vocabulary is presented in the context of information about bar coding wildlife species.

- Ask students to explain what a bar code is and where you can see them. How do they work? What are they used for?

Building Vocabulary

track 3-17

Exercise A. | Meaning from Context

- Discuss the words and ask a few volunteers to make example sentences with words they know.

- Ask students if they know other word forms related to these words such as *gene/genetic, classify/classification*.

- Play the audio at least once while students read the text.

> TIP The information in this text is summarized in the sentences in exercise B.

Exercise B.

- Explain that working out what type of word (verb, adjective, noun) is required can help students figure out the answers.

- Note that sentence 10 could be either a verb in the simple present or in the simple past.

Answer Key

1. aware	5. controversial	9. sequences
2. classify	6. sample	10. argues/argued
3. variations	7. gene	
4. technique	8. substances	

IDEAS FOR... Checking Comprehension

After listening to and reading the text, ask students to role play a short conversation between a reader who thinks bar coding sounds like a good idea and one who thinks it isn't important.

Using Vocabulary

Exercise A.

- Explain that students should try to find synonyms for each underlined word.

- Do the first item as an example.

- Suggest that students cross out the underlined word when they have written the answer.

> TIP Encourage higher-level students to try to remember the words without looking back at the text.

Answer Key

1. variation 2. sequence 3. classified
4. technique 5. substance

Exercise B.

- Encourage students to use the new words in their discussions.

- Invite volunteers to choose the question they found most interesting and present their answer to the class.

Exercise C.

- Ask students to read aloud the bar coding statistics in the box.

- Provide corrective feedback on pronunciation of large numbers if necessary.

- Encourage students to use their general knowledge to answer these questions as well as the information in this lesson.

IDEAS FOR... Expansion

- Ask students to think of different ways to help endangered species. Put students into groups. Ask each group to come up with at least five different ideas. Then pool the ideas as a class and write them on the board. Which ones are most practical, creative, effective, and easy to do?

- For homework, students can research organizations that work to help endangered species, such as the World Wildlife Fund (WWF). What kind of projects do they fund? What animals are they trying to protect?

Developing Listening Skills

45 mins

(pages 176-177)

Before Listening

Exercise A. | Discussion

- Ask students to look at the photo and describe what the scientists are doing. Ask students to discuss the questions in groups or as a whole class.

- Brainstorm a list of functions that can have positive effect on teamwork such as listening carefully, asking for opinions, and giving reasons for opinions.

Polite Expressions for Collaborating | Go over the information in the box. Practice repeating the expressions with alternative endings. For example: *Would you mind explaining that again?*

Exercise B.

track 3-18

- Explain that students should listen and check the expressions they hear.

- Play the audio. Check the answers as a class, playing the audio again and pausing if necessary.

- If time is available, play the audio one more time and ask students to note three polite expressions for agreeing (*Me too, Most likely, I agree*).

Answer Key

. . . ; don't you agree?

Could you please . . . ?

Thanks.

Listening: A Conversation about a Science Experiment

Exercise A. | Listening for Main Ideas

track 3-19

- Allow time for students to read the sentences and answer choices.

- Play the audio while students choose their answers.

Answer Key   1. a 2. b 3. a

Exercise B. | Listening for Details

track 3-19

- Read the questions aloud. Play the audio again while students take notes. Discuss the answers with the whole class.

Answer Key *(Answers may vary.)*

1. The fish in the colder water are not as orange as the fish in the warmer water.
2. There is some variation in the water temperature.
3. She handed him the fish food.
4. his notes from yesterday
5. feed the fish

IDEAS FOR... **Checking Comprehension**

Ask this additional question or write it on the board.

Why do they disagree about when to write the lab report? (*The woman wants to write the lab report as soon as possible because she has other classes to study for next week. The man thinks they need to give the experiment more time and they might get clearer results if they wait a few more days.*)

After Listening

Exercise A. | Collaboration

Remind students of the language used for collaborating.

TIP   **Write the expressions for collaborating on the board for students' reference** while they're working on the steps in exercise A.

IDEAS FOR... **Expansion**

Ask students to discuss how they would set up the experiments shown here.

- For Experiment #1, they can come up with a single hypothesis to test—temperature, amount of food available, environment.

- For Experiment #2, they should choose a plant and decide what kinds of music to play.

- For Experiment #3, they will need to choose a few different substances to test.

Exercise B. | Role-Playing   Observe students while they are talking. Give feedback on the content of their role-play as well as whether they use the expressions correctly.

Exploring Spoken English
(pages 178-179)

Grammar: Phrasal Verbs—Review

- Remind students of the information about phrasal verbs on page 158. What can they remember about phrasal verbs?

- Go over the information in the box.

Exercise A. | Meaning from Context
track 3-20

- Play the audio while students read.

- Ask them to suggest synonyms for the underlined phrasal verbs or explain their meanings.

- Ask students to cover the text and ask a few comprehension questions: *Why did Matt decide to go on the expedition? What did Matt almost do?*

Exercise B.

- Challenge students to try and complete the exercise without looking back at the conversation in exercise **A**.

- Allow time for students to write their answers.

- Go over the answers as a class. Check other meanings of these phrasal verbs in the dictionary. What other information does the dictionary give about these verbs?

Answer Key

1. turn down 2. set up 3. talk into 4. turn on
5. pick up 6. clear up

Exercise C. | Invite volunteers to read the conversation aloud to the class using appropriate intonation.

Exercise D. | Invite volunteers to read their answers aloud to the class.

Answer Key

1. talked, into 2. pick, up 3. set up 4. cleared up
5. turn on 6. turned down

> **IDEAS FOR...   Expansion**
>
> Ask students to make up mini-dialogs using these phrasal verbs. The dialogs should illustrate the meaning of the verb.
> For example:
> **A:** Did you want to give a presentation?
> **B:** No, but my teacher talked me into it!
>
> Students can perform their dialogs for the class or write them on cards for vocabulary review.

Language Function: Congratulating

Exercise A.

- Look back at the conversation on page 178 and notice the language for congratulating.

Student to Student: Congratulating | Go over the information in the box. Point out that appropriate and enthusiastic intonation is important to make these expressions sound sincere.

Exercise B.

- Give some examples of things you have done recently that you are happy about and ask students to congratulate you. For example: *I rode my bike for 10 miles.*

- Allow time for students to write their own successes.

 It is more realistic if students write true information about themselves. However, some students may not want to share this information, so encourage them to mention real but small successes. For example: *I did my laundry, and I didn't lose any socks. I'm trying to drink less coffee. Yesterday I only drank one cup.*

Exercise C.

- Ask students to work in pairs or ask them to walk around the classroom and congratulate each other.

- Recognize students for appropriate use of enthusiastic intonation.

Pronunciation Note
Foja: foy-uh

45 mins

Engage: Planning and Presenting a Research Proposal *(page 180)*

WARM-UP

Brainstorm different areas of scientific interest related to animals such as birds, reptiles, insects, mammals, and fish. Make a list of different regions and terrains of the world that could be interesting to study such as volcanoes, deserts, mountains, oceans, glaciers, and rainforests. Brainstorm a list of things students may already know something about and a list of things they would like to find out about.

Exercise A.

- Read the information in the blue box aloud.

- Help groups choose their topic by looking through the pictures and themes in this unit. They may also use topics from the list that they generated in the warm-up. Make sure that topics are complex enough to be interesting but will still be fairly easy to research.

- Remind students to use language for collaboration in their discussion. List the expressions on the board for reference.

Exercise B. | Planning a Presentation

- Remind students to make sure each person has an equal amount of information to present.

- Remind students to introduce each section with an introductory sentence such as: *Now I'm going to present our travel plans.*

- Tell students to practice the whole presentation in their group.

> **TIP** Suggest that a higher-level student in each group facilitates the planning phase so that all members have an equal amount to present.

Exercise C. | Presentation

- Ask each group to present their proposal.

- Remind students to refer to their notes by glancing at them and then looking up to make eye contact with the audience.

- Suggest that others in the class ask at least three questions after each presentation.

- You can develop an evaluation sheet like the one below to help students evaluate each other's presentations. In this chart, 1 is the lowest score and 5 is the highest score.

Presentation Evaluation Chart					
Speaks slowly and clearly	1	2	3	4	5
Makes eye contact	1	2	3	4	5
Introduces each main point	1	2	3	4	5
Well organized	1	2	3	4	5
Interesting content	1	2	3	4	5
Useful research idea	1	2	3	4	5

> **TIP** Tell students to take notes on each presentation. At the end, they can vote on the best one.

> **IDEAS FOR... Expansion**
>
> For homework, ask students to find an example of some recent interesting research related to animals or the environment. They can summarize the article, say why it is interesting or useful, and present the information during the next class meeting.

Entrepreneurs and New Businesses

Academic Track
Business and Economics

Academic Pathways:

Lesson A: Listening to a PowerPoint Lecture
Discussing New Business Ideas

Lesson B: Listening to a Case Study and
a Conversation
Creating a Commercial

Unit Theme

Unit 10 explores the topic of business and entrepreneurship as it relates to:

– starting a new business
– preparing a business plan
– how businesses adapt to changing market conditions

– developing new business ideas
– attitudes about bargaining over prices
– creating a commercial

Think and Discuss *(page 181)*

5 mins

- Have students look at the photo and discuss the three questions.

- Ask a few additional questions about tourism's effect on local economies: *What kinds of businesses depend on tourism? How does tourism benefit local communities? What are some of tourism's negative effects?*

Exploring the Theme: Entrepreneurs and New Businesses *(pages 182-183)*

15 mins

The opening spread features a photo of tulip fields in Holland as an example of a successful business enterprise.

- Ask students to look at the photos.

- Ask two volunteers to read the information aloud.

- Discuss ways in which these two businesses are similar or different.

- Go over the statistics in the box.

- Discuss the four questions.

- For question 4, you may want to ask if students know anyone who has started their own business and if so, have the student tell the class about the business.

- Make a chart with advantages and disadvantages of working for a company and working for yourself.

- Ask students to list some differences between small and large businesses.

- Brainstorm some ideas for new businesses in your area.

IDEAS FOR... Expansion

To prepare for this unit, ask students to choose an entrepreneur from their country and conduct research on how he or she started his or her business and why it became successful.

Building and Using Vocabulary *(pages 184-185)*

30 mins

WARM-UP

The Lesson A target vocabulary is presented in the context of a program that helps young people learn how to start their own business.

- Ask students to give some examples of small businesses in their country.

- Discuss some reasons why people might want to start their own business.

Building Vocabulary

track 3-21

Exercise A. | Meaning from Context

- Have students look at the photo and describe what they see. Does it look like a good place to work or study?

- Play the audio while students read.

- Note: *Injaz* means "achievement" in Arabic.

Exercise B.

- Ask students to discuss the three questions in pairs.

- Ask volunteers to share their answers with the class.

- Ask students how they would evaluate the winner of this competition.

Exercise C.

- To make this exercise more challenging, ask students to think of other words related to each word in blue. For example:

succeed → *success, successful*

Answer Key

1. created	**5.** competition	**9.** succeed
2. risk	**6.** profit	**10.** product
3. income	**7.** skills	
4. entrepreneurs	**8.** service	

Using Vocabulary

Exercise A.

- Have students compare the two photos and say how the people's jobs in the two photos might be different.

- Have students discuss some of the differences between working for a large company and owning your own business.

- Ask volunteers to read the statements aloud.

Exercise B.

- Ask students to discuss the answers in pairs. Then see if they agree with the answer choices made by business experts at the bottom of page 187.

Exercise C. | Self-Reflection

- Encourage students to be positive but truthful about their skills and abilities.

Exercise D. | Discussion

- Tell students to use examples from their past experience to support their statements.

TIP Point out that it is not possible, or even desirable, for everyone to be an entrepreneur. Some people do their best work as a member of a team or as part of a larger company.

IDEAS FOR... **Expansion**

Ask students to make a list of other skills not mentioned in this list that could be useful for starting a business. They could list personal characteristics such as being creative, hardworking, or organized. Ask students which skills they have and which skills they would like to have.

Developing Listening Skills

45 mins

(pages 186-187)

Before Listening

Exercise A. | Using a Dictionary

- Discuss how the three words could be connected and what the lecture might be about.

Answer Key *(Answers may vary.)*

1. florist: person who owns or works in a store that sells flowers

2. trade: to exchange goods or services for money

3. wholesale: relating to the sale of goods in large quantities for resale

track 3-22

Exercise B. | Predicting Content

- Read the incomplete notes with students.

- Play the first part of the audio while students complete the notes.

- Ask students to discuss in pairs what the rest of the lecture might be about.

Answer Key

borrow money, traits, adapt to changes, economy

Listening: A PowerPoint Lecture

track 3-23

Exercise A. | Listening for Main Ideas

- Go over the three possible main ideas.

- Play the audio while students choose the statement they think best conveys the main idea.

- Note: The first part of the lecture is not repeated on track 3-23.

Answer Key

Students should identify the following main idea: The Zappettinis' business has been successful because they could adapt to changes.

Note: The second statement is not made or implied in the lecture. We can infer that the third statement is true, but it is not the main idea.

track 3-23

Exercise B. | Listening for Details

- Play the audio and pause after each slide so that students have time to write the missing information.

- Check the answers at the end of the entire audio.

- Ask students to retell the main points to their partner using the notes and the pictures. Have them take turns for each slide.

Answer Key *(Notes may vary.)*

2. 1956, flower **3.** 1921, farm **4.** Growers, profits **5.** 30, farms, radio **6.** selling farmland **7.** large amounts, selling, 67 **8.** 200, world **9.** special Web sites, (entirely) online

---

IDEAS FOR... Checking Comprehension

Ask students to draw a time line showing the stages of development of the Zappettini family's business. Refer to the example on page 215 of the *Independent Student Handbook.*

After Listening

Critical Thinking | Use the questions to encourage students to evaluate the information in the lecture. They may want to discuss the benefits and disadvantages of doing business online.

IDEAS FOR... Expansion

- Ask students to role play an interview with a member of the Zappettini family about their business and how it has developed.

- If one or more students own a small business, ask them if they would be willing to be interviewed. If there's only one student, have the whole class interview him or her. If there is more than one small business owner in the class and time is limited, have each one be interviewed by a different group. Assign a group reporter to briefly summarize what the student said.

---

45 mins

Exploring Spoken English
(pages 188-190)

Grammar: The Infinitive of Purpose

Exercise A. | Prior Knowledge

- Ask students to explain the function of the infinitives in the sentences before analyzing the form.

- Students may not underline the entire infinitive phrase at this point.

> **Answer Key** *(Answers may vary.)*
>
> 1. to work for better profits
> 2. in order to persuade people to buy more flowers from California

- Go over the information in the grammar box.

- Explain that the infinitive of purpose is used to give the reason for doing something.

Exercise B.

- Allow time for students to write their answers.

- Invite several volunteers to write their answers on the board.

- Ask students to change the sentences so that they are true for them.

> **Answer Key**
>
> 2. I have to leave my house at eight fifteen in order to get to work by nine.
> 3. I eat only fruit for breakfast to lose weight.
> 4. To stay fit, I exercise three times a week.
> 5. To get a better job, Ed took three computer classes.
> 6. You should drink more water to improve your health.

Exercise C. | Self-Reflection

- Allow time for students to write their answers.

- Walk around the classroom as students are writing and ask questions about their information.

> **TIP** True answers help to make the grammar real for students and therefore more memorable. If students can't think of something to say, encourage them to make up something absurd to help them remember the grammar, such as, *I went to Antarctica to open an ice cream store.*

Exercise D. | Encourage students to find out more information about each answer from their partner.

Language Function: Speculating about the Future

- Read the examples and ask what students notice about the form and the meaning of each sentence.

- Emphasize that *could not* is not used to speculate about the future.

Exercise A.

- Ask the class for a few suggestions before students start the exercise.

- Allow time for students to complete their sentences. Encourage them to be creative.

Exercise B.

- Ask students to compare answers in pairs. They can change partners and repeat this exercise two or three times.

- Invite volunteers to write their answers on the board.

- Take a class vote on the statements that are most or least likely to happen.

Exercise C.

- Look at the photos of the four people and go over the information.

- Play the audio while students take notes. Pause after each person, if necessary.

Answer Key

Brad: next fall; might go to Italy

Yumiko: Right now, I work; in a few years; might try to start a business

Carlos: on Friday night; might go to the movies; may; and read

Paula: an art class; may visit my sister

Exercise D. | Discussion

- Check the answers to exercise **C** by writing them on the board.

Exercise E. | Self-Reflection

- Encourage students to think about both short- and long-term plans.

- Remind students to use all three modals and at least one negative. *I may not stay home this summer. I might get a job in Alaska.*

Exercise F.

- Suggest that students also ask each other about the reasons for these plans. For example:
  S1: I might take an art class.
  S2: Why are you interested in doing that?
  S1: To learn to be more visual and to do something creative.

- Students may want to take notes that they can use in exercise **G**.

Exercise G. | Discussion

- Have students in each pair present one of their partner's plans to the new pair.

- The new pair can then ask each student a couple of questions about what his or her partner has reported.

- If time allows, students can present a second plan of their partner's.

 30-45 mins

Speaking *(page 191)*

Discussing New Business Ideas

Critical Thinking Focus: Using Questions to Evaluate Information

- Go over the information in the box.

- Give an example of a business idea and invite students to ask you questions about it.

Exercise A.

- Read the questions aloud.

- Put students into groups to go over the information and discuss the questions.

- Walk around the classroom while students are talking. When you feel that students have covered the main points of each new business, give them a one-minute reminder before ending the activity.

> **TIP** Since students often have different reading speeds, you may want to read all the ads aloud as a whole class before starting the group discussions.

Exercise B. | Reporting to the Class

- Call on a spokesperson from each group to summarize the main points of their discussion.

> **TIP** An alternative way to handle exercise A is to ask each person in the group to choose one advertisement each, read it carefully, and then explain it to the group in their own words. They should explain what is new or innovative about the business that will make it a success.

Viewing: Making a Deal in Fes

30 mins

(pages 192-193)

Overview of the Video | This video is about shopping in a market in Fes.

Before Viewing

- Ask students to describe the photos.
- Ask students to look at the map and describe the location of Fes.
- Ask students to describe how shopping in a market like this one could be different from buying things in a store.

Exercise A. | Self-Reflection

- Allow time for students to read the statements individually and think about their answers.

Exercise B. | Discussion

- Ask students to compare answers in pairs.
- Check answers by taking a vote on each statement. (Students raise their hands if they agree.)
- Ask students to say which of these statements they feel are positive and why.

While Viewing

Exercise A.

3:57

- Tell students to look at the statements in exercise **A** in the Before Viewing section again.
- Tell students they may need to infer the answers from what they see in the video.
- Play the video while students underline their answers.

Answer Key   2, 3, 4

Exercise B.

3:57

- Read the statements as a class.
- Play the video again.
- Go over the answers.

Answer Key   1. busy 2. everyone 3. bargaining 4. customers 5. watch 6. buy

Exercise C.

3:57

- Read the statements as a class.
- Play the video again if necessary.
- Go over the answers.
- With the whole class, have students make the necessary changes to turn the false statements into true statements. For example: 1. Owners and customers decide the price together, by bargaining.

Answer Key   1. F 2. T 3. F 4. T 5. T

> **IDEAS FOR...   Expansion**
>
> Play the video again and ask students to write three questions about it. Have students ask each other the questions.

After Viewing

Critical Thinking

- Encourage students to evaluate the information from the video by asking additional questions: *Is bargaining an important part of your culture? Are there different bargaining styles in different cultures? What do you think of bargaining? Do you enjoy it? Why, or why not?*
- Allow time for students to discuss the questions.
- Ask a spokesperson from each group to report back to the class.

> **IDEAS FOR...   Multi-level Classes**
>
> Ask students to select one of the following activities for homework:
> - Interview a neighbor or friend about his or her shopping habits. Report the results to the class.
> - Create a survey about shopping habits and use the survey to interview five of your classmates. Report the results to the whole class.
> - Write a journal entry about where you like to shop and why.

Building and Using Vocabulary *(pages 194-195)*

30 mins

WARM-UP

The Lesson B target vocabulary is presented in the context of learning to create a business plan.

- Ask students what the purposes of a business plan are. *(Business plans provide information for banks or investors who might loan money to help start the business. Business plans also help the entrepreneur see what his or her costs might be.)*

Building Vocabulary

track 3-25

Exercise A. | Meaning from Context

- Explain that students will read about how to make a business plan.
- Play the audio while students read the text.
- Ask students which part of the advice they found the most useful. *Which part would be the most difficult to do?*

Exercise B.

- Remind students that looking at the word type (noun or verb) will help them work out the answers.
- If there is time, have students compare these definitions with those in a dictionary and find additional meanings for these words.

Answer Key 1. b 2. a 3. c 4. h 5. j 6. g 7. i 8. f 9. e 10. d

Exercise C. | Discussion

- Encourage students to use their general knowledge as well as the information in this text to answer these questions.
- Ask students to say which question they think is the most difficult to answer.

Using Vocabulary

Exercise A.

- Look at the photo and ask students to guess what kind of small business they will read about.
- Ask students to fill in the missing words without looking back at the previous page, if possible.
- Go over the answers.

Answer Key

1. borrow	5. market	9. potential
2. budget	6. customers	10. predict
3. lend	7. goal	
4. advertise	8. achieve	

Exercise B. | Encourage students to role play the interview with emotion. The interviewer sounds doubtful and cautious; Andreas sounds confident and enthusiastic.

Exercise C.

- Ask students to tell you which part of the conversation in exercise **A** corresponds to each question in the text on page 194.

Answer Key

He answered all questions except for the the final question (predicting possible problems).

IDEAS FOR... Multi-level Classes

Ask students to think of their own idea for a business. They should create a conversation similar to the one in exercise **A**. Allow students at different levels to create conversations appropriate to their level. Invite volunteers to perform their conversations for the class and take a vote on the best and most creative business ideas.

Developing Listening Skills

45 mins

(pages 196-197)

Before Listening

Prior Knowledge

- Have students look at the photo and discuss the two questions.

- Bring in some ads for beauty products and discuss how they appeal to their customers.

Listening: A Case Study and a Conversation

 track 3-26 **Exercise A. | Listening for Main Ideas**

- Elicit or explain the meaning of *case study*. Ask: *Why are case studies useful for students who are studying business?*

- Allow time for students to read the four questions. Play the audio while students take notes.

Answer Key

1. selling beauty products online
2. teenagers in small towns
3. She knows her market.
4. We can learn about business success.

 track 3-26 **Exercise B. | Listening for Details**

- Play the audio while students choose their answers and correct the false statements in their books. Go over the answers with the whole class.

Answer Key *(Answers may vary.)*

2. T
3. F (Her profits are up to $1500 a month.)
4. F (She did surveys of all her female classmates and friends.)
5. T
6. F (In the future, she will probably study business administration in college. / . . . she wants to find new products overseas. / . . . she may take a trip to Taipei. / . . . she could set up a real store in her town.)

Exercise C. | Discussion

- Ask students to discuss the questions in pairs. Encourage students to express their opinions of Jie En's business idea. Ask volunteers to share their ideas with the class.

 track 3-27 **Exercise D . |** Play the audio as many times as your students need to hear it to complete the sentences.

Answer Key

1. countries, different **2.** companies **3.** successful
4. business plan

 track 3-27 **Exercise E. |** See if students can identify the sentence without listening to the audio again. Play the audio again so students can confirm the answer.

Answer Key

3. I think she'll ask about things the different companies did to be successful.

IDEAS FOR... Checking Comprehension

Ask students to identify what aspects of Jie En's business strategy made her business a success. What general points can be learned from her experience?

After Listening

Exercise A. | Explain that predicting test questions is a good way to review information. Remind students to use a variety of question types: *wh-*, *yes/no*, multiple-choice, etc.

Exercise B. | Make a list of possible questions on the board as students dictate them to you. Discuss the likelihood the questions have of being on a test.

Pronunciation: Thought Groups

 track 3-28 Go over the information about thought groups. Play the audio and ask students to repeat the examples.

track 3-29

Exercises A and B. | Emphasize that thought groups are not fixed. They depend on how you interpret the meaning of the sentence in context.

Answer Key

2. Josh and I / are going home / after lunch.
3. She started a business last year / when she graduated / from technical college.
4. You have to speak in English / for five minutes / to pass the test.
5. There's a beautiful red bird / singing in the tree.
6. There's an article in the newspaper /about the 16-year-old girl / in Malaysia.
7. Her experiences / can teach us a lot / about business success.
8. She might study business / when she goes to college.

30 mins

Exploring Spoken English
(pages 198-199)

Grammar: The Present Perfect Tense

- Go over the information in the box. Contrast the uses of the present perfect with those of the simple past.

Exercise A. | Invite volunteers to read the sentences to the class. Ask students to explain the meaning of the present perfect in each case by referring back to the explanations in the box.

Answer Key

2. has been 3. has lived 4. has given
5. have been 6. have had

Exercise B. | Check the answers by asking students to read out each pair of sentences.

Answer Key   1. c 2. b 3. d 4. e 5. f 6. a

Language Function: Using the Present Perfect to Start Conversations

- Ask volunteers to read the dialogs in the box.

> **IDEAS FOR...   Expansion**
>
> Ask students to continue the conversations in exercise **B** using their own ideas. Point out that the next person often uses the simple past in order to speak about a specific event. For example: *What movie did you see?* Explain that the simple past is used to talk about events at specific times in the past.

Exercise A. | Brainstorming

- Ask students to brainstorm topics in pairs.
- Compare topics as a class. Ask students to suggest questions on these topics using the present perfect.

Exercise B. | Discussion

- Tell students to stand up and walk around the classroom. Signal (for example, by clapping your hands) when you want them to stop walking and talk to the nearest person. Signal again when you want them to stop talking and start walking around again.

Exercise C. | Reporting to the Class

- After all the students have spoken, give feedback on their use of the present perfect.
- Say two or three sentences that were correct and two or three that were wrong.

Student to Student: Giving Compliments

- Go over the information in the box.
- Discuss cultural and personal differences in giving and receiving compliments. Ask a few questions: *How do you respond to a compliment? What kinds of things do you usually compliment people about?*

Exercise D.

- Suggest that students write down ideas for three things they have done that they would like to be complimented on. They can show the sentences to the group.

Engage: Creating a Commercial *(page 200)*

45 mins

WARM-UP

Bring in some examples of commercials from the TV or the Internet. You could play two or three commercials and then ask students what they remember about them or what advertising techniques they noticed.

Exercise A. | Collaboration Use the situation in the box at the top of the page to briefly explain the assignment. Explain the time limits for preparing and presenting the commercial, when presentations will be made, and how presentations will be evaluated.

- Go over the information and make sure students understand the instructions.

- Explain that students are going to write a short screenplay or script for a commercial.

- Help groups to choose their product and to think of unique features that will help sell it. They can use their own ideas. They could also choose a type of service, similar to the ones on page 191.

- Remind students to use language for collaboration in their discussion. Write expressions from page 176 on board for reference.

Presentation Skills: Showing Enthusiasm for Your Topic | Present the information in the box so that students can practice it in exercise **A**. Point out that enthusiasm for a topic is also relevant to presenting academic and research topics.

Exercise B. | Role-Playing

- Help students decide what criteria they will use to evaluate the presentations. These could include creativity, humor, acting ability, and enthusiasm.

- Ask one member of each group to introduce the commercial and the background of the characters in the commercial.

Exercise C.

- Ask students to give compliments at the end of each presentation. You may want to write the expressions from page 199 on the board for reference.

- Have students give feedback on the group presentations using the evaluation criteria they developed together. Who showed the most enthusiasm? How did they show it?

IDEAS FOR...   Expansion

Instead of creating a TV commercial, each group could prepare a magazine advertisement for their product. The finished ads could be displayed on the classroom wall. Post a blank piece of paper next to each one so that students can write feedback on each other's work. Points can be given for creativity, originality, humor, etc.

CD 1

Unit 1: Staying Healthy in the Modern World
Lesson A
Building Vocabulary

Track 2   A. Meaning from Context   Page 4

The Secret to a Long Life

What's the secret to a long, healthy life? It begins with genes, but also depends on good habits. Experts studied groups of people living in places where many people live to be 100 years old—including Sardinia, Italy, and Okinawa, Japan. People in these places suffer from fewer diseases and are more likely to live to be 100 than people in other parts of the world.

Sardinia

In Sardinia, many people, especially men, live longer than in other parts of the world. In general, women live longer than men. In fact, in the United States, there are four times as many 100-year-old women as men. However, in Sardinia, an equal number of men and women live to be 100. One of the reasons may be that men have a stress-free life there. The men typically work in the hills, which provides daily exercise and helps keep them strong. The women look after the house and money. "I do the work," says Tonino, a native Sardinian. "My wife does the worrying."

Okinawa

In Okinawa, people have very low rates of cancer and heart disease compared to Americans. One of the reasons for this is *ikigai,* a Japanese word that translates to "reason for living." *Ikigai* may help prevent stress, which can cause high blood pressure. Okinawans also eat a healthy, low-calorie diet that consists of a lot of fresh vegetables. "A full plate of Okinawan vegetables, tofu, and a little fish or meat has fewer calories than a small hamburger," says Makoto Suzuki of the Okinawa Centenarian Study. "And it will have many more healthy nutrients."

Developing Listening Skills
Pronunciation

Track 3   A.   Page 6

1. Frank exercises every day. He plays sports and lifts weights.
2. There are 16 doctors and 37 nurses at the hospital.

Track 4   Word Endings -s and -es   Page 6

Examples:

leg	legs
like	likes
refer	refers

Examples:

bus	buses
surprise	surprises
exercise	exercises

Track 5   B.   Page 6

Tara: Hello, everyone, and thanks for coming. I'd like to introduce myself. I'm Tara Sorenson, and I'm a public health nurse. Public health nurses are like other nurses, but we take care of more than one person. Our job is to keep everyone in the community healthy. I know—it's a *big* job! Mostly, I do this through education. Tonight, I have 45 minutes to teach you about heart disease.

Listening: A Talk about Preventing Heart Disease

Track 6   A.   Page 7
**   B. Listening for Main Ideas**
**   C. Listening for Details**

Tara: Hello, everyone, and thanks for coming. I'd like to introduce myself. I'm Tara Sorenson, and I'm a public health nurse. Public health nurses are like other nurses, but we take care of more than one person. Our job is to keep everyone in the community healthy. I know—it's a *big* job! Mostly, I do this through education. Tonight, I have 45 minutes to teach you about heart disease. There are different kinds of heart disease, but tonight we're talking about coronary heart disease—the kind of heart disease that can cause a heart attack. Heart attacks happen when arteries or other blood vessels become too narrow. If they're too narrow, blood vessels can't bring enough blood and oxygen to the heart, and this causes a heart attack. The good news is—there are many things you can do to prevent heart disease. The first step is pretty easy—get your blood pressure checked. High blood pressure is bad for your blood vessels, and it can lead to heart disease. So, if you *do* have high blood pressure, you need to do something about it. For example, if you're overweight, losing five or 10 pounds could help lower your blood pressure. And you probably already know this—you can lose weight by eating a healthy diet and getting enough exercise. Let's talk about diet first. . . . Now, I'm not talking about a special diet where you eat only apples and lemons for a week—nothing like that! I'm talking about healthy eating habits—how you eat most of the time. According to government reports, these habits can keep your weight and your blood pressure down, and they can help to prevent heart disease. First, eat several servings of vegetables and fruits every day. Second, eat less salt and less sugar. Third, choose low-fat dairy products such as low-fat milk, yogurt, and cheese. Fourth, eat healthy protein foods such as fish and eat only small amounts of red meat. And fifth, choose whole grains when you eat foods such as bread and rice. These are things you can do every day—or at least most of the time. I know—nobody is perfect, right? In addition, these healthy eating habits can help control your blood sugar. High blood sugar is another cause of heart disease. Now, let's talk about exercise. I suggest exercising at least four days every week, for at least 30 minutes. And not just *easy* exercise. You should be breathing hard, and your heart rate should be beating faster than usual. Not *too* fast, of course, but faster than usual. This will make your heart stronger and make you healthier. Besides high blood pressure and high blood sugar, another common cause of heart disease is smoking. I guess everyone knows it's a very unhealthy habit, and if you want to prevent heart disease, you *have* to quit smoking. It's also important to get enough sleep, and to find healthy ways to deal with stress. After all, we have jobs and children and other things that make us feel stressed out. So, go for a walk or take a yoga class! Then make a healthy dinner for your family. If you do these things, you will be much less likely to have coronary heart disease in the future. Of course, some people do need medication to control their blood pressure or blood sugar, so it's important to visit your doctor regularly. All right . . . are there any questions? . . . Yes, the man in the back . . .

Exploring Spoken English
Grammar: Adverbs of Frequency

Track 7   A. Prior Knowledge   Page 8

Manuel: I always drink plenty of water before I exercise.
Jenny: I never ride my bike without wearing a helmet.
Samir: I usually warm up for five to 10 minutes before I exercise.
Monica: My friends and I often bring healthy snacks such as fruit and peanuts when we go hiking.
Erik: I always make sure to wear comfortable clothing. I don't want to be too hot or too cold.

Speaking

Track 8   C.   Page 11

Hello, my name is Megan Schwarz. To stay healthy, I exercise—but not every day. I usually exercise four or five days a week. I also take vitamins every day.

For exercise, I usually go jogging two or three times a week. . . . And I also walk, of course—I walk to class every day, actually. Sometimes I go biking, but I don't have my own bike, so I can only ride on weekends in the park. They rent bikes in the park on Saturdays and Sundays. In the future, I want to have a healthier diet. Now, I live in a very small apartment with no kitchen. I eat a lot of fast food because I can't cook for myself. After I graduate, I plan to move to a bigger apartment with a kitchen. I also want to buy my own bike, so I can bike every day. . . . Thank you very much.

Lesson B
Building Vocabulary

Track 9   A. Meaning from Context   Page 14
Allergies

What are allergies? If you have a particular *allergy* to something, you become sick, or have an *allergic reaction,* when you eat, smell, or touch it. Many people have allergies to pollen. The diagram below shows what happens when there is an allergic reaction to pollen.
1. First, pollen enters the body through the nose.
2. Second, the body's immune system responds to the pollen with IgE antibodies. These antibodies attach to a mast cell. A mast cell is a cell that usually defends your body against health problems.
3. The next time the same pollen enters the body, the IgE antibodies "tell" the mast cell. The mast cell "thinks" there is a problem and tries to defend the body.
4. When this occurs, the mast cell produces substances in the body that cause allergic reactions such as sneezing, itching, and breathing problems.

Using Vocabulary

Track 10   C. Meaning from Context   Page 15
Allergies and the Hygiene Hypothesis

Many people work very hard to keep their houses clean. But can too much cleanliness cause health problems? One theory is that dirt is good for us. Dirt on farms, for example, contains substances that exercise our immune systems when we're very young. Research shows that allergies are not common among people who live with farm animals. Of course, there are many causes of allergies. For example, if your parents have allergies, you're more likely to have them, too. The pressure and stress of modern life could be another cause. But if the hygiene hypothesis is correct, it might be a good idea to have a cow at your house—or at least not to worry so much about cleanliness.

Developing Listening Skills
Listening: An Informal Conversation

Track 11 **A. Listening for Main Ideas** **Page 16**
B. Listening for Details

Raymond: I had no idea that allergies were so serious. And so common!
Elena: Yeah, they are. I'm allergic to strawberries, peanuts, and chocolate—and I *love* chocolate.
Raymond: Wow—allergic to *chocolate*—that must be really hard.
Elena: It *is*. Are you allergic to anything?
Raymond: No, at least not that I know of. I don't really know much about allergies . . . fortunately.
Elena: Yeah, you're lucky. My allergies are really bad sometimes, especially in spring and early summer . . . *and* I also have asthma.
Raymond: Oh, you have asthma, too? It can't be easy for you living in the city with all this air pollution then, can it?
Elena: Well, the air pollution is bad, but I find it much harder to be around smoke. It's really hard for me to breathe. . . . I also can't be around cats for too long—and some kinds of flowers also cause my asthma to act up. Fortunately, my asthma medication works really quickly, and I feel better almost immediately.
Raymond: Well, that's good. What about food allergies? Those can be really bad too, can't they?
Elena: You bet. Like I said, I'm allergic to chocolate, strawberries, *and* peanuts.
Raymond: I'd *hate* to be allergic to chocolate. I can't *live* without chocolate.
Elena: Well, believe me, it's not easy, but being allergic to peanuts is actually harder because you don't always know when food contains peanuts or peanut oil.
Raymond: Yeah, that's true. Actually, yesterday in class Professor Martinez was telling us that there is a no-peanuts policy here on campus—because allergies can be really dangerous.
Elena: Yeah, that's right. The cafeteria and snack bar stopped serving foods that contain peanuts and peanut oil last year after a student had an allergic reaction and was rushed to the hospital.
Raymond: Oh, yes . . . I remember that. Professor Martinez called food allergies the "new" allergy problem.
Elena: Yeah, that's right, and she also said that there were twice as many children with food allergies in 2002 than in 1997. I think it's called the *new* allergy problem because it's growing very quickly. I read that nowadays, about six percent of children have food allergies.
Raymond: Six percent! Wow, that's a lot of kids!
Elena: It sure is!

Exploring Spoken English
Grammar: Tag Questions

Track 12 **A., B.** **Page 18**

1. John took the bus, didn't he?
2. They're tired, aren't they?
3. You called her last night, didn't you?
4. Tina likes pizza, doesn't she?
5. That man is your friend, isn't he?
6. He's late again, isn't he?

Unit 2: Energy and Our Planet
Lesson A
Building Vocabulary

Track 13 **A. Meaning from Context** **Page 24**

The Process of Global Warming

1. Our demand for fossil fuels such as oil and natural gas is growing.
2. This growing need for energy causes us to burn more and more fossil fuels.
3. Burning fossil fuels such as coal puts carbon into the air.
4. Carbon dioxide, or CO_2, and other gases reduce the amount of heat that goes out into space.
5. When less heat goes out into space, it means that more heat stays in the earth's atmosphere.
6. When more heat stays in the earth's atmosphere, the average temperature increases, making it warmer.
7. A significantly higher average temperature leads to climate change and changes to the weather.
8. Climate change can have a negative impact on people's lives. For example, climate change can make it difficult to grow food in some places.
9. People are starting to conserve energy by making changes that cause them to use less fuel.
For example, people are buying smaller cars.
10. Smaller cars are more efficient because they use less gas and oil.

Developing Listening Skills
Pronunciation

Track 14 **Stressing Key Words** **Page 26**

Where is Karen **going**?

Is the meeting in Simpson Hall?
No, the meeting is at the **Student Union** this week.

Katelyn: Are you going to the Environmental Club meeting?
Dan: Maybe. What is it about?
Katelyn: It's a presentation about energy around the world. A photographer is going to talk about different families and how they live.
Dan: Sounds interesting! What time is the meeting?
Katelyn: It starts at seven.
Dan: Is it in the science building?
Katelyn: No, it's at the Student Union this time.

Listening: A PowerPoint Lecture

Track 16   A. Listening for Main Ideas   Page 27
**   B. Listening for Details**

Well, it's just about seven o'clock, so why don't we get started. . . . So, hello and good evening everyone and thank you for coming. . . . I'm Carl Jones, and tonight I'm going to talk to you about energy use around the world. Instead of talking in general terms, I decided to focus on three families from three different countries and discuss how each family uses energy in their daily lives. Can everyone hear me OK? OK, good. First, let's look at the Chuma family, in a village in Botswana. Mr. Chuma is a tour guide and the family also raises cows. In this slide, you can see Mrs. Chuma doing some of her housework outside the family's small house. She washes her clothes by hand, and then she hangs them in the sun to dry. She isn't using any fossil fuels to wash and dry, which means she isn't sending any greenhouse gases into the atmosphere. In the next slide, you can see three of the Chumas' children and their neighbors' children going to school. The children walk there, and in the rainy season they have to use this boat to cross the river. Again, you can see they aren't using much energy, so they aren't producing much carbon. Overall, the Chumas' demand for fossil fuels is quite low. They use fossil fuels for a few important things, such as electric lights and a radio, so as a family, they have a fairly small impact on the environment. But global warming is having a significant impact on the people of Botswana, and the Chuma family is one example of this. Sometimes they don't have water . . . and there isn't enough grass for their farm animals because of the dry climate. Now, let's look at the next family—the Nelsons. . . . The Nelsons live in Las Vegas, in the United States. Here, in this slide, you can see Brandi Nelson with her laundry. She's listening to the news on a big TV while she folds laundry in their living room. She washed and dried these clothes in a machine, and there are many other things in their house that use electricity. In the next slide, you can see the Nelson children coming home from school. They attend a private school. The Nelsons drive them to school

because there isn't a bus. Brandi and her husband are entertainers, and they both drive to their jobs because it's faster than public transportation. Their jobs are far from their home, so they use about a gallon of gasoline every day. The Nelsons want to conserve energy, and have done several things to help reduce the amount of energy they use. For example, this year they bought more efficient appliances. They also want to put in a solar energy system in their house, but it's *very* expensive. Their lifestyle puts a lot of carbon into the atmosphere, but they say it's difficult to change their habits. . . . Finally, we have the Panchal family. This is Neetu Panchal, who lives in Jaipur, India. There are 11 people in her family, all living in one house. They have a washing machine, but she hangs her clothes on the top of her house to dry. The Panchals are saving money to build another room in their house for Neetu's cousin and his wife. Neetu's sister, Lalita, goes to work by bus. Here she is in this next slide here. . . . Lalita works in a hotel far from their home. It takes her 40 minutes to get there. She hopes that the family will soon buy a car, so she can spend less time getting to work and more time at home with her family. India has a *very* big middle class—more than 300 *million* people. Changes in the lifestyles of India's middle class will have a big impact on the world's greenhouse gases. For instance, by 2050, there will be about 600 *million cars* in India—more than any other country in the *world* . . . and as the demand for cars increases, so will the demand for oil and gas.

Lesson B
Building Vocabulary

Track 17   A. Meaning from Context   Page 34

Tips for Saving Energy and Protecting Our Environment

Scientists believe that the earth's temperature is increasing. They believe this increase in temperature is having a negative impact on our environment. You might think that protecting the planet is too big a job for you, but it isn't. There are many small and practical ways you can conserve energy and help protect the environment. Here are some helpful tips. Cut back on driving by taking public transportation or walking more often. You will save a lot of gas if you drive to work two or three days a week instead of five! Shop at local stores close to your home. You will drive less, so you can spend less money on gas and more money on food. Turn off lights and electronics when you aren't using them so you don't waste electricity. Replace your old appliances like refrigerators and dishwashers with new, efficient models. Old appliances consume more energy than new ones. Keep track of the electricity and gas you use and how you use it. Write down the different activities you do that use gas or electricity and how often you do them in an energy journal. Use your energy journal to help you set a lower target for your energy use each month. For example, if your energy bill is $100 one month, try lowering your bill to $80, or by 20 percent the next month. Try to reduce the amount of energy you use by making gradual changes to your lifestyle. You will see that making small changes each month can have a big impact on the amount of energy you use—and help protect our beautiful planet!

Developing Listening Skills
Pronunciation

Track 18   Using Intonation to Show Feelings   Page 36

Our energy bill is 200 *dollars* this month.
Our energy bill is *200* dollars this month.

Track 19   A., B.   Page 36

1. **Speaker A:** The earth's temperature might increase by five degrees.
   Speaker B: The earth's temperature might increase by five degrees.
2. **Speaker A:** Americans produce twice as much carbon as Europeans.
   Speaker B: Americans produce twice as much carbon as Europeans.
3. **Speaker A:** Oh, you bought a new TV.
   Speaker B: Oh, you bought a new TV.

Listening: An Informal Conversation

Track 20   A. Listening for Main Ideas   Page 37

Daughter: What's the matter, Dad? You look kind of upset. . . .
Father: Well, I *am* kind of upset. Our energy bill is *very* high this month.
Son: Really, how much is it?
Father: It's 400 dollars, which is a *lot* higher than usual.
Son: Wow—that sounds like a lot!
Father: Well, it *is* a lot. I'd really like to find ways to cut back on how much energy we use.

Track 21   B. Listening for Details, C.   Page 37

Son: Well, we can help think of some ideas . . . like last week in school we learned about energy-efficient light bulbs. Maybe we should get some of those?
Father: Well, that's a start. Thanks, Jason . . . I'm sure our local hardware store sells them, or maybe even the grocery store.
Daughter: I have an idea—Jason should take shorter showers. He takes really long showers and that probably wastes *a lot* of energy!

Son: I do not! You take longer showers than I do. Maybe you should stop using your hair dryer every morning. That probably uses a lot of electricity, and it's noisy.
Daughter: I don't use it *every morning*.
Father: Kids! You don't have to start taking short showers or stop using the hair dryer, but we do need to try to reduce the amount of energy we use. I think we should keep track of how we're using energy every month—you know, write it down. . . . Then we can set a target—for example, maybe we try to decrease the amount of energy we use by 10 percent next month.
Son: How are we going to do *that*?
Father: Well . . . we can all try to think of ways to cut back. . . . What do you guys think we can do?
Son: I know! We can put in solar heating panels!
Father: Well, that might save energy, but solar panels are expensive. That's an interesting idea, Jason, but let's try to think of little things we can do every day. Changes we can start making immediately.
Daughter: Well, OK . . . for one thing, we have three computers here at home—so, we should try to remember to turn them off at night. That could help.
Father: Good idea, Diana. OK, let's try to think of some more ideas. You kids have some good ones.
Daughter: Oh—maybe we can try to use some of our appliances, like the stove and oven less often.
Son: What—you want us to eat cold food every day?
Daughter: No! I didn't say that, but maybe we should eat sandwiches or salads for dinner sometimes instead of cooking every night. Cooking probably uses *a lot* of energy.
Father: OK, kids. . . . That's a good idea, Diana, but I don't think we have to stop eating cooked food for dinner. We just need to think more carefully about how we're using energy and make some changes, and they can be small, gradual changes. Let's see . . . for example, this month we can replace our light bulbs with more energy-efficient ones and remember to turn off our computers at night—those were two great ideas you kids had. Then next month we'll look at the bill and see how much we've saved. Then we can decide what to do next. Sound like a plan?
Son: Yeah!
Daughter: Uh-huh!

Unit 3: Culture and Tradition Lesson A
Building Vocabulary

Track 22   A. Meaning from Context   Page 44

1. Women in Japan still wear a kimono for their wedding. They haven't stopped wearing these beautiful clothes.

2. In Korea, people eat traditional food such as rice cakes on New Year's Day. They have done this for a long time.

3. We are developing a program to teach foreigners about our culture. Now we are making plans for this program.

4. In my country, we have a custom of giving money to children on their birthdays. We usually give them money.

5. In the future, many languages might disappear. No one will speak these languages.

6. A group of people called the Inuit live in the cold regions of the world. They live in cold areas.

7. The Navajo people use storytelling to help preserve their language and traditions. They use storytelling to keep their language and traditions.

8. Some kinds of animals, such as tigers, are endangered today. They might all die.

9. Scientists estimate that there are over 7000 languages in the world. They don't know the exact number.

10. Television is a factor in cultural change. It is a cause of these changes.

Developing Listening Skills

Pronunciation

Track 23   Reduced Function Words   Page 46

Examples:
I hear the phone ringing.
There's a message for Molly.
What are you reading?

Track 24   B.   Page 46

Professor Daley: One of the oldest traditions in North and South America is the cowboy. As you know, cattle eat grass—a *lot* of grass—so a herd must be moved often to new places with more grass. The people who move them are called cowboys.

Listening: A Lecture

Track 25   A. Listening for Main Ideas   Page 47
B. Listening for Details
C. Making Inferences

Professor Daley: OK, so let's continue. . . . A lot of people today think that the last cowboys disappeared a long time ago. It's true that there are fewer cowboys today, and the cowboy way of life is endangered. Money is a big factor here. Cowboys usually don't make a lot of money for all the hard work they do, so fewer young people today want to be cowboys—it's not an easy lifestyle. Even so, in some parts of the world, cowboys still ride their horses, watch the cattle,

and practice traditional cowboy customs. A few years ago, a photographer named Robb Kendrick traveled around different regions of North America talking to modern cowboys and taking photographs with a very old kind of camera. He recorded their way of life in a book called *Still: Cowboys at the Start of the Twenty-First Century.* Here are two of the cowboys that Robb Kendrick included in his book. This is Tyrel Tucker—he was 18 years old when Kendrick took this photograph. Tyrel was working on a ranch at that time. He was born in Wyoming, in the United States, and he was riding horses before he could walk. He got his first horse when he was two years old. He worked as a cowboy during his school vacations. Then his mother needed help with the family ranch, so he left school at the age of 17. He was happy to do that. . . . Tyrel was working outside while all his classmates were indoors playing computer games. His most difficult job was one winter when he and his older brother worked alone on a ranch in Arizona. He estimates they took care of *2300* cattle there, so it was a big job! Every day from December to April, they rode their horses on over 150 square miles of land . . . an area the size of a major city. Can you imagine that? And there were no other people there. Tyrel and his brother lived in a shack with no electricity and ate the same food every day: pancakes, sausages, potatoes, and hamburgers. Tyrel enjoyed the work and developed a love for being outdoors. . . . Now let's take a look at the cowboys of Mexico. The cowboy tradition started in Mexico in the 1600s, when Spanish people brought the first cattle to the New World. Big ranches needed workers to take care of their herds of cattle. These men were called *vaqueros,* from the Spanish word *vaca,* which means cow. The *vaqueros* started wearing big hats to keep the sun off their faces and high boots to protect their legs. Later, some Mexican *vaqueros* moved north into Texas, and their clothes became a part of the cowboy culture there. Wearing cowboy hats and boots is part of the culture that is still preserved today in Texas and other parts of North America. Today Mexico has two kinds of cowboys. One kind called *charros* ride horses and compete in sports. The other are the *vaqueros* that I just described, and who work with cattle on the ranches, especially in the north of the country. The *vaqueros* still ride horses and live outdoors for many months at a time. This is a picture of Manuel Rodriguez, a young *vaquero* in Coahuila, Mexico. Manuel started helping his father at La Mora Ranch when he was only four years old. He was the fourth generation of his family to work at La Mora Ranch. Manuel recently got married and moved to the city, but he plans to move back to the countryside and work as a *vaquero* again after his first child is born. OK, so from this we can see that the cowboy's way of life hasn't changed. That's because the work hasn't changed. Cowboys still ride horses because they can get close to the cattle. Herds of cattle still need a lot of grass, so cowboys must keep moving them from one place to another. That's the job of the cowboy. It's the same today as it was in the past.

Exploring Spoken English
Language Function: Asking for and Giving Clarification

Track 26 A. Page 48

Emily: You said that Mexico had the first real cowboys. Are there still cowboys today?

Professor Daley: Yes, there are. They're workers who live with the cattle and take care of them. Some ranches are very large and cattle need to be moved from place to place, so yes, there are still cowboys.

Li: You also talked about two kinds of cowboys in Mexico. Could you explain that?

Professor Daley: Sure. The most famous cowboys in Mexico are the *charros.* They ride their horses in contests called *charreadas.* The other kind of cowboys are the *vaqueros*—the ones who work with cattle every day.

Li: I still don't understand.

Professor Daley: Let me explain. Some Mexican cowboys do it as a hobby, and others do it as a job. For the *charros,* it's mostly a sport, or a hobby. For the *vaqueros,* it's their work.

Li: So, what you mean is that Manuel Rodriguez is a *vaquero,* and not a *charro.*

Professor Daley: Exactly!

Emily: Do you mean that *charros* aren't really cowboys?

Professor Daley: No, *charros* are a part of the tradition, but many of them don't do it as actual work. What I mean is, they are cowboys—but it isn't a job.

Lesson B
Building Vocabulary

Track 27 A. Meaning from Context Page 54

Anthropology 106: Culture and Music

Assignment: Oral Presentation

For this assignment, you will select a kind of music from another country and teach your classmates about it. You should plan to do the following in your presentation: Describe how the music sounds. Does it have a nice melody that's easy to listen to? Is the rhythm fast or slow? What kinds of instruments do the musicians play? Does the music typically have lyrics? Are the lyrics usually happy or sad? Play an example of the music for your audience so they can hear it. Explain where and when people typically listen to this kind of music. Do they listen to it at weddings or on special holidays? Compare this kind of music to another kind of music you know about. How are they similar? Then contrast the two kinds of music. How are they different? Define any words you think your classmates may not know. In your conclusion, summarize the most important ideas of your presentation. Answer any questions and remember to thank your audience. Your presentation should be at least two minutes.

Developing Listening Skills
Listening: An Assignment and a Student Presentation

Track 28 A. Note-Taking Page 57

Professor: OK. . . Yesterday we listened to music from Latin America. We heard some traditional music, and we also heard new music that developed from this traditional music. Now I'm going to ask *you* to do some research and give a short presentation to the class. In this presentation, you're going to do six things, so please take notes. First, I want you to select a kind of music from another culture to present. Then I want you to talk about the culture it comes from—got that? Next you should describe the music and explain which aspects of this music are traditional and which aspects are new, or modern. Then, I want you to compare and contrast it with another kind of music we have talked about in class this semester. I'd also like you to play a sample of the music if you can. And finally, you should briefly summarize the main ideas of your presentation and answer any questions from your classmates. OK? Everyone got that? You'll give your presentations in class next Thursday and Friday. Now, if everyone is clear about that, I'd like to . . .

Female student: Excuse me, I have a question. How long should our presentations be?

Professor: Right, that's important! I want you to talk for at least two minutes.

Male student: I have another question—what do you mean by *aspects*? You said we should explain what *aspects* of the music are traditional.

Professor: I mean things like the instruments, the rhythm, the melody, or the lyrics. OK, see you next Thursday. . . .

Track 29 B. Listening for Main Ideas Page 57
C. Listening for Details

Male Student: Good morning. . . . I'm Alex, as you know. I'm going to talk to you today about music from the Roma culture. The music I selected is by a group called Shukar Collective. They're from Romania. First, I just wanted to define the word *Shukar,* which means "fine" or "really good" in Romany. I think they're really good, so I think it's a good name for them. Shukar Collective is a group of musicians and DJs from Eastern Europe, and they play music from the Roma culture. About their culture . . . traditionally, the Roma didn't have a home, so they often moved from place to place. Now they mostly stay in one place, and many of them speak two languages—their own Roma language, and the language of the country where they live. One thing the Roma people are very famous for is music. Traditional Roma music usually has a very fast rhythm, and the lyrics show very strong feelings. The traditional Roma instruments are drums and an instrument called the *cimbalom* . . . that sounds sort of like a piano. . . . They also use some new, electronic instruments, so their music is a mixture of traditional and modern sounds. I *really* like their music . . . as you can probably tell. Shukar Collective is made up of three traditional singers and four electronic musicians. They call their music electro-gypsy-dance . . . and it's very popular in dance clubs all over Europe. I actually did not bring a sample to play today, but I can bring one in tomorrow—or you can probably go online and find some of their music. OK, to summarize—Shukar Collective is a group from Eastern Europe. They play music from the Roma culture, which combines traditional and new, electronic sounds. It is very popular in Europe. Well, that's it. Thanks for listening to my presentation. So . . . does anyone have any questions?

Unit 4: A Thirsty World
Lesson A

Building Vocabulary

Track 30   A. Meaning from Context   Page 64

Water: What do you know?

1. Brazil has more fresh water available for its people than any other country.
2. Farmers require 911 gallons (3450 liters) of water to produce 2.2 pounds (1 kilo) of rice.
3. Clean water is very important for staying healthy. About one million people die each year from drinking dirty water.
4. Melting snow and ice is a fast and easy way to provide drinking water for people in cold places.
5. China has built more than 22,000 dams to manage water for different uses such as electricity.
6. Scientists say that 13 gallons (50 liters) of water per day is enough for one person.
7. You can collect water in a desert with just a sheet of plastic and an empty can.
8. Water is a renewable resource, so we can use the same water again and again.

9. The Nile River in Africa (the longest river in the world) flows through four different countries.
10. People in Australia use the smallest amount of water of any country in the world.

Developing Listening Skills
Listening: A Guest Speaker

Track 31   A. Listening for Main Ideas   Page 66
B. Listening for Details

Dr. Paul Benjamin: Well good afternoon everyone and thank you for taking the time to be here today. I'm Dr. Paul Benjamin. I'm an engineer and I—I'm here to talk to you about the Three Gorges Dam in China. As you probably already know, China's Three Gorges Dam is one of the world's largest dams. It's 1.4 miles long and 607 feet tall. That's *five* times larger than the Hoover Dam in the United States. The dam's reservoir is 410 miles long—it's *huge*. So, as you can—as you can imagine, an engineering project of this size requires a lot of workers—and a lot of workers were involved in the building of the Three Gorges Dam. At one time, more than 26,000 Chinese workers and foreigners were working together to build the dam. . . . OK, so why was the Three Gorges Dam built? Why was it constructed? Well, it was—it was constructed in order to provide a renewable source of energy for China's increasing demand for electricity—that's one reason. It was also built to help control the water in the Yangtze River. The water from this river is a valuable resource, but if it's not managed well, it can be very dangerous. Chinese authorities estimate that in the 20th century about 300,000 people were killed in the Yangtze River floods. Protecting people's lives is a priority, and the dam was designed to protect people by controlling the river and preventing future floods. OK, now another reason the dam was built was for . . . was to help China's economy. Because the dam makes the water in the Yangtze River deeper, larger ships can travel farther up the river. This means more trade, so more money—a better economy. So, we can see that building an enormous dam like this can provide important benefits. But at the same time, there are risks . . . potential problems. For example, the Three Gorges Dam will put a lot of land under water. Many towns and villages will probably disappear. Over one million people have already lost their land and have had to leave the region to find new homes. The dam will also put many very old historical and cultural sites under water . . . which is very unfortunate because China has such an interesting history. In addition, a huge engineering project like the Three Gorges Dam can have a significant impact on the environment. For example, factories flooded by the dam's reservoir are polluting the river, making the water very dirty and unsafe. Also, the dam can cause an increase in erosion, or the gradual destruction of soil and rock near the river. Earthquakes are another concern in this area. An earthquake that occurs near a dam that controls so much water could be extremely dangerous. OK, so in conclusion, the Three Gorges Dam is one of the world's largest dams. It was built to provide important benefits to the people of China. But as we can also see, there are some significant risks to building a dam this large. The main thing is to understand that there are both benefits and risks to this kind of enormous engineering project. Well, it looks we are just about out of time. So again, thank you all very much for coming today. . . . Now, are there any questions?

Pronunciation

Track 32   Syllable Stress   Page 67

Examples:
enough
resource
interested

Track 33   A.   Page 67

1. available
2. significant
3. information
4. understand
5. vocabulary
6. pronunciation
7. difficult
8. important
9. necessary
10. conservation

Track 34   B.   Page 67

1. The water from this river is a valuable resource.
2. But if it is not managed well, it can be very dangerous.
3. Another reason the dam was built was to help China's economy.
4. Many towns and villages will probably disappear.

Lesson B
Building Vocabulary

Track 35   A. Meaning from Context   Page 74

Australia's Water

Water is important in any country, but in Australia, it is the most important resource. Australia is the driest continent in the world, and water is very scarce in many regions. The normal amount of rain in some places is only 1 inch (25 millimeters) per year. Several years ago, the rain stopped falling in Australia, and many parts of the country soon experienced a drought—a time of extremely dry weather. Children in some towns have never seen rain in their whole lives. It was a crisis for the entire country, and many people were very worried. The government had to decide how to allocate water for different uses. Rules were made about domestic use of water for things such as gardens, swimming pools, and showers. Some water is also needed for industry because the country makes cars, ships, and machines. But Australians' main use of water is for agriculture. Farms produce rice, grapes, oranges, cattle, and many other foods, and these require a lot of water. Instead of rain, Australia uses water from rivers and underground reservoirs for farming. Some parts of Australia have had more normal amounts of rain recently, but in many places there, the crisis continues. And with the earth's climate getting hotter, other countries will face urgent decisions about water use like Australia has.

Developing Listening Skills
Listening: A Group Discussion

Track 36   A. Listening for Main Ideas   Page 76
**   B. Listening for Details   Page 77**
**   C. Note-Taking**

Student 3: For our presentation on "how people are affected by drought," here's some information about drought in a region called the Murray-Darling Basin. That's the biggest agricultural area in Australia. The city of Adelaide is there. In some places in the region, it hasn't rained once in seven years—can you imagine?
Student 2: Wow! That's unbelievable!
Student 3: I know. . . . The article has some really good photos—maybe we can show them to the class. Look, here's one of a farm family. Their name is Adlington.
Student 1: They sure don't look happy. What does their farm produce?
Student 3: Milk. They used to have 500 cattle, and now they only have 70 because grass is so scarce.
Student 2: Really? Wait a minute. . . . In class, Professor Larsen said that river is used for irrigation in Australia—what's it called? The Murray River?
Student 3: Yeah, that's right, but the normal water level of the river is now extremely low. The government allocated most of the water to the city of Adelaide for domestic use and to big industrial farms. The law says that some water has to stay in the river, for the fish and animals, so there's not much left for agriculture.
Student 1: Well, in my opinion, water is the most important resource a place has. And cities are the top priority. I mean, that's where most people live.

Student 3: And here's a picture of a lake in another part of Australia that's almost disappeared called Lake Boga. Look at this. . . . Now all the water in Lake Boga is used by farmers.

Student 1: That's unbelievable. It's totally gone!

Student 3: The article said Lake Boga used to be a vacation place. Now it's in crisis. No one stays in the hotels, and the whole town smells like dead fish.

Student 2: Ugh! That's really sad . . . but I think growing food is the most important consideration.

Student 3: Look . . . this photo shows an urgent meeting for rice farmers, talking about how the government reduced their water allocation—the guy in the middle, Frank Whelan, started one of the first rice farms in Australia, in 1962. The article says Australia used to grow a million tons of rice a year, but now they only grow 21,000 tons.

Student 2: You're kidding! And the world needs a lot more food.

Student 1: Hmm . . . but doesn't rice need a lot of water to grow? Maybe Australia isn't the best place for rice farms.

Student 2: That just doesn't sound fair. It seems like the farmers have to give *their* water to industry and everyone else.

Student 3: Not exactly. There are a lot of water rules and restrictions in Australian cities, too. For example, the article says that water is collected in showers and used to water gardens.

Student 1: Seriously?

Student 3: Yeah.

Pronunciation

Track 37   Suffixes and Syllable Stress   Page 77

Examples:

educate	education
allocate	allocation
present	presentation
conserve	conservation

Track 38   A.   Page 77

1. industry   It's a big industrial city.
2. agriculture   He studied at an agricultural college.
3. government   She works for a governmental agency.
4. describe   The description of Lake Boga was very interesting.

 CD 2

Unit 5: Inside the Brain
Building Vocabulary

Track 2   A. Meaning from Context   Page 84

Facts to Make You Think about Your Brain

1. Every time you have a new thought or recall a memory, your brain creates a new connection or pathway.

2. Even without words, you can understand when someone is happy, sad, or angry. There is a small area in your brain called the *amygdala* that helps you "read" other people's faces and understand their moods.

3. The belief that we only use a tiny amount (10 percent) of our brains is false. Each part of the brain has a function, so we use 100 percent of our brains.

4. Learning something new can change the structure of the brain in just seven days. If you want to change your brain quickly, you should try learning a new skill like juggling or playing a musical instrument.

5. The things you do, eat, smell, and touch every day all generate thoughts. The average person experiences approximately 70,000 thoughts a day.

6. Your brain is an amazing, complex organ. It contains more than 100 billion neurons that are always sending messages. But not all neurons are the same—different neurons send messages at different speeds.

7. Every time you think, laugh, or sneeze, it's because chemical signals are moving from neuron to neuron. Your brain is a very powerful organ. In fact, when you are awake, your brain generates between 10 and 23 watts of electricity—or enough power to power a light bulb.

8. The hypothalamus is the part of your brain that controls your body temperature. It knows your correct body temperature (98.6 degrees Fahrenheit/ 37 degrees Celsius). When you get too hot, it makes you sweat. When you get too cold, it makes you shiver.

Developing Listening Skills
Listening: A Documentary

Track 3   A.   Page 86
B. Listening for Main Ideas
C. Listening for Details

Your *Amazing* Brain. . . .You carry around a three-pound organ in your head that controls everything you will ever do. It enables you to think, learn, create, and feel emotions, and controls every breath and heartbeat—this fantastic control center is your brain. It is so amazing that a famous scientist once called it "the most complex thing we have yet discovered in our universe." Your brain works faster than a supercomputer. . . . Imagine your cat is on your kitchen counter. She's about to step onto a hot stove. You have only seconds to respond. By using the signals coming from your eyes, your brain quickly calculates when, where, and how quickly you will need to move to stop your cat from stepping on the stove. Your brain then tells your muscles what to do. You run across the kitchen, and pick your cat up, and she's safe. No computer can come close to your brain's ability to receive, process, and respond to the enormous amount of information coming from your eyes, ears, and other sensory organs. The brain is also an amazingly powerful organ. It generates enough electricity to power a light bulb. Your brain contains about 100 billion microscopic cells called *neurons*—so many it would take you over 3000 years to count them all. . . . Whenever you dream, laugh, think, see, or move, it's because tiny chemical and electrical signals are moving at high speed between these neurons along billions of tiny neuron highways. The activity in your brain never stops. Thousands and thousands of messages are sent around inside your brain every second. Your neurons create and send more messages than all the phones in the entire world. And while a single neuron generates only a tiny amount of electricity, all your neurons together can generate enough electricity to power a light bulb. Your neurons are not only able to send lots of messages, they are able to send them very quickly. Neurons send information to your brain at more than 150 miles per hour. For example, imagine that a bee lands on your bare foot. Sensory neurons in your skin send this information to your spinal cord and brain at a speed of more than 150 miles per hour. Your brain then uses motor neurons to transmit, or send, the message back, through your spinal cord telling your foot to shake the bee off quickly. Motor neurons can transmit this information at more than 200 miles per hour. What about learning? We know that learning increases knowledge, but studies show that when you learn, you actually change the structure of your brain. For example, an activity like riding a bike seems impossible at first. But soon you master it. But how do you do this? As you practice, your brain sends "bike riding" messages along certain pathways of neurons over and over, forming new connections. In fact, the structure of your brain *changes* every time you learn, as well as whenever you have a new thought or memory. Exercise also has an impact on your brain. Research shows that exercise actually helps make you smarter. It is well known that any exercise that makes your heart beat faster such as jogging or playing soccer is good for your body and can even help improve your mood. But scientists have recently learned that for a period of time *after* you've exercised, your body produces a chemical that makes it easier for your brain to learn. . . . So the next time you're stuck trying to solve a homework problem, go out for a bike ride or go jogging, then try the problem again. You just might discover that you're able to solve it.

Pronunciation

Track 4   Linking Sounds   Page 87

Consonant sound → Vowel sound
It's a fascinating job.
Vowel sound → Vowel sound
I knew it was the right answer.
The book will certainly be interesting.
Consonant sound → Same consonant sound
What was your reason for being late?

Track 5   Collaboration   Page 87

1. Your brain controls everything you do.
2. Your brain generates enough energy to power a light bulb.
3. The activity in your brain never stops.
4. Your brain sends a message to your foot to shake the bee off quickly.
5. Any exercise that makes your heart beat faster can help your mood.
6. Your body produces a chemical that makes it easier to learn.

Lesson B
Building Vocabulary

Track 6   B. Meaning from Context   Page 94

Romantic Love vs. Long-Term Attachments

There are many different kinds of love. There is the strong emotion we feel when we fall in love. There is the attachment between parents and children, and the quiet feeling of security that develops slowly in long-term relationships, when couples are together for many years. Your brain knows the difference between romantic love and other attachments. When we're in love, the amount of a brain chemical called *dopamine* increases. This increase in dopamine gives us the extra energy we feel when we're in love. At the same time, this increase in dopamine can make the brains of people who are "lovesick" similar to the brains of people with OCD—Obsessive Compulsive Disorder. People with OCD cannot stop thinking about something, and these thoughts can cause compulsive behaviors—actions the person cannot control, such as washing their hands again and again. Similarly, people who are in love often cannot stop thinking about the person they are in love with. Both people with OCD and people in love may sometimes find it difficult to function normally in their daily lives because of their thoughts. Fortunately, this "lovesickness" is a short-term condition. With time, strong romantic feelings decrease, and we can concentrate on "real life" again. As time passes, couples have higher levels of oxytocin—a brain chemical connected with calm feelings of happiness and trust. So is love only a matter of brain chemistry? In fact, while chemicals do affect the way we feel, psychological factors are also important. We might be attracted to someone who likes the same things we like, for example, or someone who makes us feel safe and secure.

Developing Listening Skills
Before Listening

Track 7   A.   Page 96

Cathy: Did you understand everything Professor Wong said yesterday about short-term memory?

Toshi: Yeah, I think so.

Cathy: I'm not sure that I did.

Toshi: Well, here's what I got from the lecture: Your short-term memory only lasts a few seconds, right? Information enters the brain through the senses—things we taste, touch, smell, and so on . . . and we remember it long enough to function normally.

Cathy: Sorry . . . but what do you mean by "function normally"?

Toshi: Well, for example, if I ask you a question, you can remember the question long enough to answer it.

Liz: Right, but you might not remember the question tomorrow.

Listening: A Conversation between Students

Track 8   A. Listening for Main Ideas   Page 97
             B. Listening for Details

Cathy: Did you understand everything Professor Wong said yesterday about short-term memory?

Toshi: Yeah, I think so.

Cathy: I'm not sure that I did.

Toshi: Well, here's what I got from the lecture: Your short-term memory only lasts a few seconds, right? Information enters the brain through the senses—things we taste, touch, smell, and so on . . . and we remember it long enough to function normally.

Cathy: Sorry . . . but what do you mean by "function normally"?

Toshi: Well, for example, if I ask you a question, you can remember the question long enough to answer it.

Liz: Right, but you might not remember the question tomorrow.

Cathy: OK, that makes sense, but how is the process similar or different for "long-term memory"?

Toshi: Actually, the process is quite different. First of all, to create a long-term memory, your brain has to decide that something is important.

Cathy: Like information from yesterday's lecture?

Toshi: Right . . . or how to ride a bicycle.

Liz: Sure—like both of those things. But there's more to the process. To learn new information, you have to concentrate—you know, really focus on it and think about it—or study it. Or to learn how to *do* something, like ride a bicycle, you have to do it again and again.

Cathy: Yeah. . . . So, in other words, if I want to memorize information for, say, an exam, and have it go into my long-term memory, I need to really concentrate on the information when I hear it or read it, and maybe review it several times. That's just common sense, I think.

Toshi: It *is* common sense, but it's interesting to me that when you learn new things, your brain forms new connections—new pathways of neurons.

Cathy: That *is* interesting. So learning actually *changes* the structure of the brain.

Unit 6: What We Eat
Lesson A
Building Vocabulary

Track 9   C.   Page 104

1. Today many countries have produced guidelines to teach their citizens about healthy diets.
2. Most doctors recommend eating a lot of fruits and vegetables.
3. Fresh fruits such as oranges and bananas contain important vitamins.
4. You should eat a few servings of protein every day. Fish, meat, and tofu all contain protein.
5. Cheese is an excellent source of calcium; so are milk and yogurt.
6. Scientists believe that the regional food in Sardinia helps the people who live there live long, healthy lives.
7. It's OK to include some sweets such as chocolate in your diet, but not too many.
8. Some scientists believe that eating broccoli can improve your memory. I'm going to eat some before the test next Friday!
9. Bananas only grow in specific areas of the world. They can only grow in countries with warm, tropical climates such as Costa Rica.
10. On an average day I drink three cups of coffee but yesterday I drank five.

Developing Listening Skills
Pronunciation

Track 10   Intonation of Finished and Unfinished Sentences   Page 106

I have to go to the supermarket.
She lives in Tokyo.
I saw Pam yesterday . . .
Mike's brother called . . .

Track 11   A.   Page 106

1. I really don't like milk.
2. Rick has two brothers. . .
3. For dinner, we had chicken . . .
4. On my next vacation, I want to go to Chile.
5. My mother is a teacher . . .
6. On Saturdays, we usually go to the park.

Listening: A Seminar

Track 12   A. Listening for Main Ideas   Page 107
             B. Listening for Details

Mi-Ran: Hello, everyone. . . . As you know, I'm from South Korea, a country that developed very quickly.

Fifty years ago, it was an agricultural country. Today, it's one of the most modern countries in Asia, with many high-tech industries. And people's diets have modernized, too. In my research, I've been looking at these changes in diet . . . and trying to answer this question: Which kind of diet is better—a traditional diet or a modern one? Okay, this chart shows what Koreans ate every day in two different years: 1969, before Korea started modernizing, and 1995, after Korea was modernized. You can see that in 1969, people were eating about 37 ounces of food every day, and in 1995, they were eating about 39 ounces of food. That's not a very big change. So, even before Korea was modernized, overall, people had enough food.

Male student: Mi-Ran, may I say something here? Um, you're talking about the average amount of food. . . . So, that means some people had more than that, and some people had less . . . so maybe there were people who really didn't have enough to eat.

Mi-Ran: That's a good point. Actually, because Korea was a farming country then, everyone had *some* kind of food, but it wasn't always a healthy diet. OK, moving on . . . when we compare the kinds of food people ate, we see a significant difference. The most important food in Korea is rice—we eat it three times a day. In 1969, people were eating 20 ounces of rice every day—more than a pound! That's a lot of rice. But in 1995, they were eating only 11 ounces of rice and other grains per day—much less than in the past. Now, remember, the total amount of food increased during that time. So, what *were* people eating? If you look at the chart, you'll see that people were eating more of everything. The amount of vegetables increased a little—from nine and a half ounces a day in 1969, to 10 ounces a day in 1995. But people were eating a *lot* more fruit. The amount of fruit people ate increased from about two ounces a day to about five ounces a day. And look at meat. . . . In 1969, people were eating only a very tiny amount of meat—about a quarter of an ounce a day. In 1995, they were eating almost two and a half ounces of meat a day. Finally, look at the last numbers—for milk. OK, for milk, in 1969, people were only drinking about one-tenth of an ounce of milk per day. In 1995, that increased to about 2.3 ounces a day.

Female student: Could I ask a question, Mi-Ran? Is that just milk, or does that include other dairy products, too?

Mi-Ran: Actually, that includes all dairy products. A lot of Koreans love yogurt and ice cream.

Track 13   C.   Page 107

Mi-Ran: To continue. . . as the country developed, instead of just eating a lot of rice and vegetables, Koreans started including many other kinds of

foods in their diets . . . especially animal products like meat, fish, eggs, and dairy products, which were expensive. One reason for this change was that people had more money, so they could buy more of these expensive foods. The percentage of animal products in the Korean diet went from three percent in 1969 to almost 21 percent in 1995! That is the biggest change in the Korean diet. Now, a lot of experts recommend that your overall diet should be mostly plant foods such as fruits and vegetables. They believe that animal products aren't healthy. But I want to tell you about one more interesting change in Korea. Young people today are much taller now than their parents were. The average height of teenage boys is about three and a half inches taller than 20 years ago. And the average teenage girl is almost 2 inches taller. It's very interesting! Young people now are much taller because of the improved diet. If children eat more protein, they grow up to be taller. Really, everyone in Korea is healthier now. If people include more fruit in their diets, they get more vitamins. So . . . in conclusion, in some other students' reports, we heard about places where changing to a modern diet has caused many new health problems. But this information about Korea shows us that sometimes, a modern diet can be better than the traditional diet. Thank you very much. Does anyone have any questions?

Lesson B
Building Vocabulary

Track 14   A. Meaning from Context   Page 114

1. This bar graph shows how much fruit people eat in one country. The *y* axis represents the number of servings of fruit. The *x* axis represents age groups. Each apple represents one serving. You can see that teenagers don't eat very much fruit.

2. This line graph shows how the amount of sugar people eat in one country has changed. The numbers are the yearly amounts of all kinds of sugar eaten by one person. The line illustrates how much the use of sugar has increased. The last point shows that in 2000, each person ate almost 152 pounds (69 kilograms) of sugar!

3. This pie chart shows how the average family in one country spends the money in its food budget. The biggest section, or slice, is for meat and fish, and the smallest section is for "others"—things such as salt and cooking oil.

4. This diagram explains what people should eat for a healthy diet. The labels tell you how many servings of each type of food people should eat every day.

Developing Listening Skills
Listening: A Group Discussion

Track 15   A. Listening for Main Ideas   Page 117

Katie: Okay, ready? So, who has a suggestion for our guidelines?

Nicole: Well, we could tell people about fast-food places that do have some healthy food.

Omar: But that's not what people usually eat there. I think we should just talk about regular fast food, like fried chicken . . .

Leah: Yeah, good idea. Hey, do you know what I read? The average person in this country eats fast food twice a week.

Katie: You're kidding! That's way too often, especially for children.

Nicole: Yeah, I think so, too. . . . Maybe our guidelines should tell people how often it's okay to eat fast food.

Katie: Well, what does everyone think about that?

Steve: That sounds like a good idea.

Omar: Yeah, I think so, too.

Nicole: Me, too.

Leah: Yeah, sounds good.

Track 16   B. Listening for Details   Page 117

Katie: Okay, so now we have an idea for our guidelines. We only have five minutes left, so we'd better hurry. So, how often *is* it okay to eat fast food?

Leah: Well, from what we learned in class, fast food almost always has too much salt and fat to be healthy. Remember those bar graphs we looked at?

Steve: That's true. But if we say that people should *never* eat fast food, they won't listen.

Nicole: Maybe we should say this: It's okay to have a fast-food meal any time, if you eat something healthy with it like a salad or fruit.

Omar: So, three cheeseburgers and an apple is a healthy meal?

Leah: I know! What about this as a guideline? If the rest of your diet is good, you can enjoy fast food occasionally.

Katie: Okay, but what do you mean by occasionally? We should explain that.

Leah: Oh, for example, once a week.

Nicole: No, that's way too often . . . what about once a month?

Steve: Yeah, that sounds a lot better to me. If people usually eat a healthy diet, one fast-food meal in a month won't be a problem.

Leah: Yeah, you're right, that's better.

Katie: Omar, what do you think?

Omar: Once a month? That sounds okay.

Katie: Great! So, in summary, we've decided people should not eat fast food more than once a month.

Steve: Right . . . so what kind of visual should we use to show our guidelines?

Omar: What about a pie chart?

Katie: A pie chart—that's a great idea.

Steve: Right, we could label each section with different kinds of food, or food groups, like vegetables and fruit.

Katie: Great idea! Next we need to write our guidelines on the board . . .

Leah: Here, I can do that.

Katie: Thanks, Leah. I really appreciate it. My writing is so hard to read.

Leah: No problem!

Track 17   C.   Page 117

1. I think we should just talk about regular fast food, like fried chicken . . .
2. Maybe our guidelines should tell people how often it's okay to eat fast food.
3. But if we say that people should *never* eat fast food, they won't listen.
4. If people usually eat a healthy diet, one fast-food meal in a month won't be a problem.
5. Next we need to write our guidelines on the board . . .

Unit 7: Our Active Earth
Lesson A
Building Vocabulary

Track 18   A. Meaning from Context   Page 124

Inexpensive Buildings for Earthquake Zones

The earth's crust consists of several different pieces called tectonic plates. These plates are always moving. The places where the earth's plates meet are called boundaries. When the plates push together they can form mountains. Some of the plates jump as they move. When these plates jump, they can cause earthquakes. Places where earthquakes are more likely to occur are called earthquake zones. Haiti and Chile are examples of countries in earthquake zones. In 2010, strong earthquakes occurred in Haiti and Chile. The earthquake in Haiti killed more than 200,000 people, but in Chile, fewer than 1000 people died. So why did more people survive the Chilean earthquake? One difference is the buildings. In Chile and in other developed countries, buildings are constructed from stronger materials. For example, concrete walls are reinforced with steel rods. In countries such as Haiti, heavy walls and roofs are usually not reinforced. This is dangerous because in an earthquake, buildings shake and they can collapse on top of the people inside. Engineers in several countries are working to solve the problem. Better buildings can be constructed cheaply. The engineers hope that in the future, more people will survive earthquakes.

Developing Listening Skills
Listening: An Earth Science Lecture

Track 19   A. Listening for Main Ideas   Page 126
            C. Note-Taking   Page 127

Okay, so today we're going to continue talking about plate tectonics. As you know, the earth's crust consists of several plates. There are 14 major plates plus many smaller plates. These plates are always moving, of course, and exciting things happen as a result. The places where the earth's plates meet are called boundaries . . . and there are three main boundary types. The first are called *convergent* boundaries. There, plates come together. This pushing together can cause mountains to form. One plate can also move under another at a convergent boundary, making the mountains on the top plate rise even higher. In fact, the highest mountains on Earth—the Himalaya—are the result of a convergent boundary. The second type of boundary is called *divergent*. At a divergent boundary, the plates move apart. As they move away from each other, a body of water can form between them. A good example of this is the Persian Gulf region, where the Arabian Plate and the Eurasian plate moved apart to form the Persian Gulf and the Gulf of Oman. More recently, the two plates have become convergent again, forming the mountains in Iran. You don't have to worry about the gulf disappearing, though, because these changes take place over millions of years. Okay, the third and final type of boundary is called a *transform* boundary. There, the plates are moving past each other. . . . To give you an example, along the San Andreas Fault in California and northern Mexico, one plate is moving north while the other plate is moving south. The plates don't move smoothly, however. The movement only happens occasionally, when the plates move in small or large "jumps." And when the plates make a *big* jump, the result is a major earthquake.

Lesson B
Building Vocabulary

Track 20   B. Meaning from Context   Page 134

The Gatekeeper of Merapi

Mbah Marijan has a very unusual job. He's the Gatekeeper of Merapi, an active volcano on the island of Java in Indonesia. According to traditional stories, an ogre named Sapu Jagat lives inside Merapi. The gatekeeper knows the mountain better than anyone, and his job is to keep the ogre quiet, or else tell people when the volcano will become dangerous so that they can evacuate. It's an important job because many people live near Merapi. Marijan's own village of Kinarejo is only three miles (five kilometers) from the volcano, and the city of Yogyakarta, where 500,000 people live, is just 20 miles (32 kilometers) away. In fact, more people live near active volcanoes in Indonesia than in any other place in the world. On the island of Java alone, there are 30 volcanoes and 120 million people. One of the world's best-known natural disasters occurred in Indonesia in 1883. The eruption of Mount Krakatau, a volcanic island near Java, caused a tsunami that killed more than 36,000 people. In addition, there was enough volcanic ash from the eruption to affect the earth's weather for several months. Active volcanoes are dangerous; however, people live near them because volcanic soil is very rich. In Kinarejo, most people are farmers. For them, living near Merapi means making a living. Evacuating means leaving behind their homes, animals, and lives—at least for a while. So, as long as the gatekeeper says it's safe to stay, the villagers of Kinarejo won't leave.

Developing Listening Skills
Pronunciation

Track 21   Syllable Stress Review and Syllable Number   Page 136

Examples:
collapse
survive
dangerous
materials

Track 22   A.   Page 136

1. according (to)
2. active
3. affect
4. disaster
5. eruption
6. evacuate
7. make a living
8. natural
9. villager

Listening: A Group Discussion

Track 23   A. Listening for Main Ideas   Page 137
            B. Listening for Details

Richard: I'm really glad we're doing this. Studying alone never works well for me.
Ann: I agree. I think studying in a group is really helpful, especially for an exam. Should we talk about the questions we have?

Richard: Definitely. For instance, I don't understand the difference between lava and magma. Aren't they the same thing?

Tony: They *are* the same thing—melted rock. But when it's *inside* the earth, it's called magma, and when it comes *out* of the earth, it's called lava.

Richard: According to Chapter 6, that's right. Now, who can explain why volcanoes are dangerous?

Tony: Yeah, Professor Lopez said that hot lava can kill people and start fires. He also talked about huge rocks and hardened lava. I wouldn't want to be nearby when those fly out!

Ann: Did anyone understand the part about the man in Indonesia? Isn't it okay if he tells people when it's time to evacuate?

Tony: It might be okay, but it's not very scientific. The U.S. government told everyone to evacuate before Mount Saint Helens erupted. Geologists had said the volcano was going to erupt, so almost everyone left, but some people stayed. When it erupted, 57 people were killed, so knowing when to evacuate *is* very important.

Ann: Wow, I guess it does make a difference.

Richard: I think you're missing something about that man in Indonesia. The gatekeeper's an important part of village culture. It's a tradition to listen to him.

Ann: Right. That's a good point.

Exploring Spoken English

Grammar: Gerunds as Subjects and Objects

Track 24   B. Note-Taking   Page 138

Hasan: Hello, I'm Hasan, and I'm from Bangladesh. I'm a soil scientist. I work at helping farmers to get the most from their land. I also teach them to take care of the land for future generations. Farming is very important in Bangladesh, and fishing is, too. Every year, we get heavy rains and flooding, making the soil here very rich.

Margaret: My name is Margaret. I live in a small village near Glarus, Switzerland. My family makes a living by keeping cows. You've probably heard of Swiss cheese—it's famous all over the world. Our farm is in the mountains, and that means moving the cows several times a year. It's a lot of work.

Cecilia: Hi, I'm Cecilia from Havana, the capital of Cuba. I'm a high school student. Here in Havana, the weather is great most of the time, so spending a lot of time outside is normal for us. I love walking in Old Havana, getting something to eat there, or just spending time with my friends. We're on the ocean, so going to the beach is everyone's favorite pastime.

 CD 3

Unit 8: Ancient People and Places
Lesson A
Building Vocabulary

Track 2   A. Meaning from Context   Page 144

It's not often that the vice president of Guatemala visits an archaeological site, but that's what happened when William Saturno, an archeologist, found a very old Mayan mural. The mural showed the beauty of Mayan painting. Saturno discovered the mural inside a room that was once next to a pyramid. The mural room and pyramid were later covered by a larger pyramid—part of the ancient Mayan city known as San Bartolo. At first, Saturno could only see a small part of the mural. He had to dig through earth and stone in order to reveal the rest. Then, instead of using a camera, Saturno used his scanner to take digital images of the mural. He took about 350 scans! The mural wasn't the only important find at San Bartolo. The archaeologists also uncovered a royal tomb. There, the bones of a Mayan king were buried, with objects such as a bowl in the shape of a frog and an image of the Mayan rain god Chac.

Developing Listening Skills
Pronunciation

Track 3   A., B.   Page 146

Did you see the tomb?
Is the professor going to meet with him?
Where is the pyramid?
How many people went on the trip?

Listening: A Guided Tour

Track 4   A. Listening for Main Ideas   Page 147
B. Listening for Details

Tour Guide: Good morning, and welcome to Uxmal! This is one of the most popular Mayan historical sites in Mexico, and for good reason. Uxmal has several pyramids and other structures from the Late Classic period, that's AD 600 to AD 900. I think they're the most beautiful of all the Mayan ruins. Maybe you'll agree with me after the tour. The guided tour takes about 90 minutes, but after that you can stay here until closing time if you want to. Okay, let's get started. The first stop on our tour is this huge pyramid right behind me. It's called the Magician's Pyramid, and it's unusual because it has *rounded* sides. . . . Most pyramids have *flat* sides.

We don't really know the Mayan name for this pyramid, or for any of the structures here at Uxmal. But there is an old story that a magician built this pyramid in *one night*, which is why we call it the Magician's Pyramid. We don't know exactly how long it really took to build the pyramid, but what we *do* know is that it was built in *five* different stages, so really—it took *hundreds* of years to build. Okay, let's walk over to the ball court. After that, we'll go to the Governor's Palace. In front of *that* structure is something very special. It's called the Jaguar Throne. As you may know, a jaguar is a wild cat, and you can still find a few wild jaguars today. Okay, so the Jaguar Throne looks like a jaguar with two heads. In the middle was a kind of *seat*—for a very important person of some kind. Now, here we are at the ball court. Who can tell me about the ball games that were played in this ball court? Anyone?

Exploring Spoken English

Grammar: The Passive Voice with the Past

Track 5   D.   Page 149

The New Seven Wonders

Bernard Weber wanted to use modern technology to bring the people of the world closer together. He knew that the original Seven Wonders of the Ancient World were chosen by one person. Six of the wonders don't exist anymore. So he created a way to let the world determine the New Seven Wonders: an open election using the Internet and text messaging. Anyone could nominate a special site, and anyone could vote. Naturally, many people voted for sites in their own countries. In some places, people were encouraged by their government to vote. On the other hand, sites in 220 countries were nominated, so there were plenty of wonders to vote for. Millions of votes were registered, and on July 7, 2007, the seven winners were announced in Lisbon, Portugal. Fourteen finalists were also announced—perhaps because it was difficult to limit the Wonders of the World to only seven.

Lesson A and B Viewing: The Lost City of Machu Picchu

Track 6   C.   Page 152

The city of Machu Picchu was built by the Incas high in the Andes Mountains in what is now Peru. The Inca civilization lasted from around AD 1100 to around AD 1500, when the Spanish conquistadors arrived in South America. After the Incas were defeated by the Spanish, few people knew about Machu Picchu. Then in 1911, an English explorer named Hiram Bingham found the city. At that time, it was a very quiet place. Today, Machu Picchu is a popular destination for tourists. Some people worry that the visitors will damage the historical site. Other people say that tourism brings money into an area that very much needs it.

Lesson B
Building Vocabulary

Track 7   A. Meaning from Context   Page 154

New Clues about Tutankhamen: His Life and Death

In 1922, Howard Carter found the remains of a young man in a tomb filled with royal treasures from ancient Egypt. Newspapers around the world reported the discovery and described the gold jewelry, precious stones, and beautiful art found in the tomb. Everyone wanted to know who this important man was. We now know Tutankhamen was the son of Akhenaten, and he ruled Egypt from 1332–1322 BC. He became pharaoh as a child, and he died young. On the other hand, many questions are still unanswered. Was Tut ill? Was he murdered? What did he look like when he was alive? In 2005, scientists began to analyze Tut's remains with computer tomography (CT) and modern forensic medicine—a science usually used to solve murder cases. Tut's remains were scanned in a CT machine, which created 3-D images. Using this technology, scientists were able to determine that Tut was probably not murdered and was about 19 when he died. Scientists also worked with an artist to create a lifelike model of Tut. Not everyone likes the result, however. People disagree about his race, but according to the CT scans, he probably looked a lot like modern Egyptians.

Lesson B
Developing Listening Skills
Listening: A Conversation between Students

Track 8   A. Listening for Main Ideas   Page 156
**   B. Listening for Details   Page 157**
**   C. Making Inferences**

Silvio: Hey, Laura. I'm really glad you had time to get together. I'm having trouble with an assignment in my communication class.
Laura: What's the assignment?
Silvio: We have to give an oral summary of a movie or TV documentary. I watched a cool documentary about an archaeological site in Vietnam.

Laura: That sounds interesting.

Silvio: It was interesting, but the problem is—I don't really know how to summarize.

Laura: Hmmm . . . are these your notes?

Silvio: Yeah. I wrote down a few things while I was watching.

Laura: Actually, they look pretty good. In a way, you did some summarizing already.

Silvio: I did?

Laura: Sure. You didn't write down every word you heard, right? Everything in your notes looks pretty important, or at least interesting.

Silvio: Okay. So what do I do now?

Laura: Well, you could try a technique that newspaper reporters use. Let's call it the "*wh-* questions technique for summarizing."

Silvio: Sounds good! How does it work?

Laura: It's easy. You ask yourself *who, what, when, where, why,* and *how.* For instance, who was involved in the documentary you watched?

Silvio: The Vietnamese government, mostly. And some archaeologists.

Laura: Good! And what happened? Or what did the people do?

Silvio: Okay. I think I get it.

Laura: The idea is to identify the important information, and to *start* with that information.

Silvio: That makes sense. But what about information that's less important? Like all of these things the archaeologists found?

Laura: Actually, a few supporting details can make a summary stronger. I mean—it's one thing to say that they found some old stuff. But if you can support that with a few examples . . .

Silvio: Right—I see. Well, I'm going to give a great oral summary! Thanks for the help, Laura!

Laura: Any time. Oh—and don't forget to practice. Then I can guarantee you'll do well.

Unit 9: Species Survival
Lesson A

Building Vocabulary

Track 9   A. Meaning from Context   Page 164

The Beagle in South America: The *Beagle* expedition's priority was to map the harbors and coastlines of South America. Charles Darwin spent a lot of his time on land, exploring parts of Argentine Pampas, the Atacama Desert, and the Andes Mountains.

Argentina, 1832: At both Punta Alta and Monte Hermoso, Darwin found many fossils of large prehistoric animals. He could not identify the fossils, but they were similar to modern animal species from the area. This might have been the beginning of the idea that modern species could change over time from earlier species.

Chile, 1833: In South America, the men on the *Beagle* sometimes ate a South American bird called a *rhea.* In Patagonia, Darwin heard about a smaller type of *rhea.* It lived mostly in southern Patagonia, while the larger *rhea* lived in northern Patagonia. The two species were separated by the Rio Negro. At this time, Darwin became interested in the diversity of animal life. Could an animal's environment affect traits such as size?

Galápagos Islands, Ecuador, 1835: Here, Darwin began to develop his ideas about why and how the diversity of species occurred. In a process he called natural selection, an animal with a useful trait was more likely to survive, and therefore more likely to reproduce. The animal's offspring would then inherit the useful trait. In contrast, animals of that same species with a different trait might die and not reproduce. In this way, a species would adapt to its environment and change over time.

Developing Listening Skills
Before Listening

Track 10   Note-Taking   Page 166

Lecturer: Many people know the story of Charles Darwin and the voyage of the *Beagle.* But some of the story is—in fact—legend. First of all, it was a *long* voyage. It lasted for over five years. And Darwin did not go directly to the Galápagos Islands. He was in South America for over three years before he ever went to the Galápagos. Now, most people *do* know that Darwin's ideas about how animals change and adapt began on the *Beagle* voyage. Darwin saw that modern animals looked a lot like prehistoric animals, so he thought that modern animal species actually changed and adapted from those prehistoric species. He was right about that. When the ship arrived in the Galápagos, Darwin saw the amazing diversity of animal life there. As a result, he began to think about ways the environment affects animals, and that led to his ideas about the process of natural selection.

Listening: A Biologist's Talk about Birds

Track 11   B. Using a Graphic Organizer   Page 167

Biologist: All right. Let's stop here for a moment. One type of bird I *know* we're going to see today is the finch. These birds are very common here in the UK as well as in many other parts of Europe. Oh, good. Look over there. Do you see the bird on that plant? It's a goldfinch. Unlike other finches, the male goldfinch has a very long beak, so it can get the seeds from inside those flowers.

Female Student 1: Excuse me. Is that a male or a female goldfinch?

Biologist: It's definitely a male. The female's beak is shorter, so she can't get seeds from that flower. Are there any other questions?

Male Student: Yes. Is the goldfinch here all year?

Biologist: Actually, most of them fly to warmer parts of Europe in September or October. They come back to the UK in the spring. Okay. Let's talk about a second type of finch—the greenfinch. The greenfinch has an even wider range than the goldfinch. It lives in most parts of Europe, and also in northwest Africa and parts of Turkey.

Female Student 1: Is there anything else that's special about the greenfinch?

Biologist: I'm glad you asked that question. . . . The greenfinch is interesting because it has a large, strong beak. It uses that powerful beak to break open larger seeds.

Male Student: So, the male goldfinch eats the small seeds inside flowers, the female goldfinch eats other small seeds, and the greenfinch eats the larger seeds.

Biologist: That's exactly right. Each bird has found a way to have its own special place in the environment. If many other birds eat *small* seeds, and you're the only bird that eats *big* seeds, then you'll always have plenty to eat.

Female Student 2: I have a question. Does the greenfinch leave in the winter like the goldfinch does?

Biologist: Most of the time, no. They stay here, but you will find them living in different places during different seasons. In the summer, you're more likely to find them in parks and forests. But in the winter, when there is less food, you'll find them in people's gardens and in farmers' fields. Remember, they have those large beaks, so they can eat the seeds and grain crops that people leave behind. OK, let's continue on . . .

Exploring Spoken English
Pronunciation

Track 12   A.   Page 168

banana   demand   answer

Track 13   Full and Reduced Vowel Sounds and Secondary Stress   Page 168

Examples:
banana   develop   awake

Examples:
local   factor   season

Track 14   B.   Page 168

1. practical
2. attachment
3. proportion
4. compare
5. available
6. support

Track 15   C.   Page 168

1. recommend
2. atmosphere
3. romantic
4. classify
5. quantity
6. disappear

Language Function: Explaining Causes and Effects

Track 16   A.   Page 170

The Process of Natural Selection

Here's a brief explanation of the process of natural selection. First, the environment affects animals in some way. Because of this, the animals that have certain helpful traits do well in their environment . . . and therefore, they survive and reproduce. The offspring of these animals inherit the helpful trait from their parents. Then these offspring grow up, reproduce, and pass the helpful trait onto *their* offspring and so on and so on. This process continues and, as a result, most of the animals in the species have the helpful trait.

Lesson B
Building Vocabulary

Track 17   A. Meaning from Context   Page 174

Bar Coding Life on Earth

Paul Hebert is a biologist at the University of Guelph in Canada. But as a young man back in the 1970s, part of his job was to classify thousands of different species of moth. Finding tiny variations in the moths in order to describe each species scientifically was not easy, however. Then, in 2003, Hebert suggested something a bit controversial. Instead of using descriptions to identify different species, why not use their DNA? Hebert argued that a bar code—similar to the bar codes on products in a store—could be created for every living thing on earth. Hebert suggested using a part of a gene called *CO1* to create bar codes. This gene is made up of four chemical substances known as *G, T, C,* and *A*. Nearly every form of life has the CO1 gene, but the sequence of the *G, T, C,* and *A* substances differs for each species. Using bar codes, scientists can identify or classify a plant or animal by testing a sample of its DNA. Not everyone agrees with Hebert's ideas. Some people argue that research money should be used in other ways. Hebert says the bar code technique is a good way to identify species because it is making the public more aware of biodiversity. Some people have even sent him samples of plants and animals to identify from their own backyards!

Developing Listening Skills

Before Listening

Track 18   B.   Page 176

Bobby: I'm glad you had time today to work on our project.
Sandra: Me, too. It's due in a week and a half, after all. I think we're going to get a pretty clear result, don't you agree?
Bobby: Most likely. The fish in the colder water are not as orange as the fish in the warmer water.
Sandra: I agree. I know it's hard to keep the water exactly the right temperature in this lab, but you *can* see the difference in the fish.
Bobby: Yeah, we've had some variation in the water temperature, especially at night. Could you please hand me the fish food?
Sandra: Here you go.
Bobby: Thanks.

Listening: A Conversation about a Science Experiment

Track 19   A. Listening for Main Ideas   Page 177
B. Listening for Details

Bobby: I'm glad you had time today to work on our project.
Sandra: Me, too. It's due in a week and a half, after all. I think we're going to get a pretty clear result, don't you agree?
Bobby: Most likely. The fish in the colder water are not as orange as the fish in the warmer water.
Sandra: I agree. I know it's hard to keep the water exactly the right temperature in this lab, but you *can* see the difference in the fish.
Bobby: Yeah, we've had some variation in the water temperature, especially at night. Could you please hand me the fish food?
Sandra: Here you go.
Bobby: Thanks.
Sandra: No problem. So, I think we should write our lab report as soon as possible. I have other classes to study for next week.
Bobby: Yeah. Me, too. But I'm afraid I don't agree. We can't write the report yet because we need to give the experiment more time. Maybe we'll get clearer results if we wait a few more days.
Sandra: OK. I see your point. Are these the notes you took yesterday?
Bobby: Yep.
Sandra: Do you mind if I copy them? I can't seem to find my notebook.
Bobby: Go right ahead, but you might not be able to read my writing.
Sandra: Oh, come on! Your writing isn't that bad!

Bobby: And could I ask you for something? Would you mind feeding the fish tomorrow? I have classes all day plus soccer practice in the evening.
Sandra: I can do that. And maybe the difference in the fishes' color will be more obvious tomorrow.
Bobby: I hope so!

Exploring Spoken English
Grammar: Phrasal Verbs Review

Track 20   A. Meaning from Context   Page 178

Matt: Jessica? It's me!
Jessica: Matt! It's great to hear your voice! Are you back in Australia now?
Matt: Yes, and I really missed you, but I'm so happy you talked me into going on the expedition! I can't believe I almost turned down such a great opportunity.
Jessica: Tell me all about it!
Matt: Well, we were high up in the Foja Mountains. No human beings have ever lived there!
Jessica: How exciting! Did you get a lot of work done?
Matt: We did! We set up a tent as our laboratory. It was small, but fine.
Jessica: Did it rain a lot?
Matt: Every day. Well—one afternoon the sky cleared up for a while, but the clouds were back by that evening. It was OK, though. The frogs didn't mind the rain.
Jessica: Oh, tell me about the frogs!
Matt: Can you believe there are 350 frog species in New Guinea? The best time to find them is at night. When I turned on my flashlight, I could see them easily and pick them up with my hands.
Jessica: That sounds great! But wasn't it scary in the forest at night?
Matt: Not really. It was fun and very interesting.
Jessica: It sounds like a good trip.
Matt: It was, and the lead scientist was really happy with my work.
Jessica: That's great! Congratulations, Matt!

Unit 10: Entrepreneurs and New Businesses
Lesson A
Building Vocabulary

Track 21   A. Meaning from Context   Page 184

INJAZ and Entrepreneurs

For university graduates in Egypt, finding their first job is a serious problem—it usually takes five years. Students say that there aren't enough jobs. But employers say that university graduates don't have the right skills to work in business or government offices. A group called INJAZ is working to change this situation. Every year, INJAZ has a competition that teaches Egyptian students how to run a business. Teams of students make plans, start their own small companies as entrepreneurs, and try to earn a profit. At the end of the competition, a group of Egypt's top business leaders choose the best company. INJAZ was adapted from an American program called Junior Achievement. Last year, nine teams in Cairo competed in the program. Some teams decide to sell a service. For example, Ahmed Youssry's company collected and recycled paper and glass from large businesses. Other teams developed a product. Nour Rafaat's company created a magazine for teenagers called *Did you know?* And Abdulhameed Ahmed's company created a special bag for carrying laptop computers. The back of the bag is hard, so you can also use it as a "lap desk" for your computer. Starting a business always means taking a risk. The students must borrow money to start their companies and pay it back from the company's income. And only one team can win the prize. Last year, the judges chose Abdulhameed Ahmed's computer bags—they even bought some of the bags. But every INJAZ team is a winner because they learn the skills they need to succeed in business.

Developing Listening Skills
Before Listening

Track 22   B. Predicting Content   Page 186

Professor: We've been talking about small businesses, and we've seen that small businesses have some disadvantages. It's more difficult for them to borrow money, and the attitude and personality traits of independent business people can sometimes make a business fail. But they also have one big advantage. It is much easier for a small business to adapt to changes in the world and in the economy. In today's class, we're going to look at how one family business has adapted and changed for success, from 1921 until the present . . .

Listening: A PowerPoint Lecture

Track 23   Pages 186–187

Professor: Okay . . . so here in this slide we have a vendor at the San Francisco Flower Mart. The San Francisco Flower Mart is one of the five wholesale flower markets in the United States. Florists come here to buy the flowers that they will use in their products. The market, or mart, opened in 1956, and you can still find many of the same kinds of flowers

here—like roses, irises, and lilies. You'll also find some of the same people—like Bill Zappettini, one of the market's flower traders. Zappettini's father came to the United States from Italy in 1921 and decided to start a flower farm. He took a big risk, but he was a skilled farmer, and the family business was very successful from the beginning. California is the perfect place to grow flowers, as we can see in this slide. The weather is warm and sunny, and there is water available for the fields. Later, the Zappettinis joined with other flower growers and formed the San Francisco Flower Growers Association in 1926, to work for better profits. The Zappettinis' farm did well even in the 1930s. Most people had very low incomes then, but they still bought flowers. Bill Zappettini says that when life is difficult, people "want to buy a little goodness and happiness to put on the table." I think I agree with him on that. Okay . . . then, in the 1960s, Bill Zappettini moved into a new area of business— flower distribution. They began shipping flowers from 30 different farms in California to markets all around the United States. Bill Zappettini even had a daily radio show. In order to persuade people to buy more California flowers, he talked about flowers as a part of everyday life—not only for special days like holidays and birthdays. In the 1980s, the economy of California began to change. . . . The area around the Zappettini farm became famous as Silicon Valley—the center of high-tech industry. Many companies wanted to buy land there to build factories and office buildings. So, for a time, the Zappettinis went into the business of selling farmland to high-tech companies. Well, that was fine for a while, but Bill Zappettini missed working with flowers, so he went into flower trading—buying large amounts of flowers from growers and selling them to flower shops. In the past, the Zappettinis bought and sold flowers only from California. But larger airplanes and improved refrigeration made it possible for flowers to travel much longer distances in good condition. We can see people loading boxes of flowers onto a plane in this slide. Today, 67 percent of the flowers in the United States are imported from countries such as Colombia, Ecuador, and Costa Rica. Bill Zappettini now sells 200 different varieties of flowers, from countries around the world, and the San Francisco Flower Mart is like a global shopping mall for flowers. "There's no way the old, traditional family farms can compete," he says. But small businesses like his have been able to adapt and change. So, now, what about the future? Some people believe that within the next 10 years, the wholesale flower market may move away from places like the San Francisco Flower Mart to special Web sites. If that's true, we can be sure the Zappettinis will adapt once again. The next Zappettini business could be entirely online. They might click to buy 10,000 orchids in Singapore—and click five minutes later to sell 2000 orchids in New York!

Exploring Spoken English

Language Function: Speculating about the Future

Track 24   C.   Page 190

Brad: I haven't taken a vacation in two years, so next fall, I might go to Italy. I'd really like to go to Rome and see the Colosseum.

Yumiko: I work for a big company in Kyoto, but in a few years, I might try to start a business with my brother.

Carlos: I don't know what I want to do on Friday night yet. I might go to the movies, or I may stay home and read.

Paula: I'm trying to decide what to do this summer. I'm a teacher, so I have three months off. I may take an art class, or I may visit my sister in Australia for a few weeks.

Lesson B

Building Vocabulary

Track 25   A. Meaning from Context   Page 194

Why YOU need a business plan!

A business plan is your map to success. In it, you write down what you hope to achieve in your new business and how you will do it. Your business plan should answer the following questions:

Your New Business
1. How big is the market for your service or product? How many people might be interested in it?
2. Who will your customers be? Teenagers? Young families? People who use computers?
3. How will you advertise your business and products to reach these people? Will you advertise online? In newspapers? On TV?

Your Money
4. What is your budget for your new business? How much money will you need for a store or office, a Web site, a computer, and other equipment?
5. How much is the potential income from your business? How much money do you expect to earn in the first three years?
6. Do you have enough money to start your business, or will you have to borrow money? Who might lend you this money? A bank? Family or friends?

Your First Year
7. What do you want to achieve in your first year? For example, is your goal to sell 1000 pizzas, or to have 10 new customers every week?
8. What problems do you predict in the first year? What action can you take to solve or prevent these problems?

Developing Listening Skills

Listening: A Case Study and a Conversation

Track 26   A. Listening for Main Ideas   Page 196
B. Listening for Details

Okay, let me give you an example of someone who started an interesting business and did an excellent job of collecting information about her market. Here's an article in the newspaper . . . about a 16-year-old girl in Malaysia named Jie En. Now, Jie En lives in a small town, and she's a high school student, and after school she runs an online business to sell beauty products to teenagers in small towns in Malaysia. Every day when she gets home from school, she goes online to check for new orders. Then she packages the products that people ordered and takes the boxes to the post office herself. It's a lot of work—but her profit is up to 1500 dollars every month! Not bad, huh?! Jie En's secret is that she knows her market very well. Before she started, she did surveys of all her female classmates and friends to collect information. She asked if they would buy beauty products online and about beauty products they couldn't find in their towns. And she recently hired an assistant to answer questions from customers while she's in school. With all this information about her market, Jie En can predict exactly what her customers want to buy. Jie En is very proud of her business. After she finishes high school, she will probably study business administration in college. She also wants to find new products overseas, and she may take a trip to Taipei. In the future, she could set up a real store in her town. Her experiences can teach us a lot about business success . . . so, let's discuss this . . .

Track 27   D., E.   Page 196

Student 1: So, do you think this will be on the test?

Student 2: Don't ask me! I *always* study the wrong thing for tests. Last time I spent hours and hours memorizing that whole list of business vocabulary, and it wasn't even on the test. So for all my hard work, I got 75 percent.

Student 1: That's really too bad.

Student 3: Oh, no, I'm sorry to hear that.

Student 1: I think she might ask about the countries she talked about and how things are different in each place. Egypt, the United States, Germany—where else did she talk about?

Student 2: Hmmm . . . And she may ask us about the names of all those companies and their owners. We really ought to memorize those.

Student 3: Actually—in my opinion—I don't think the names are so important. I think she just talked about them to give us examples.

Student 2: Then what *should* we study?

Student 3: She's been talking a lot about what makes a business successful. I think she'll ask about things the different companies did to be successful.

Student 1: Yeah . . . you're right. I think that will definitely be on the test.

Student 2: So, what did they do?

Student 3: Well, the flower company changed and adapted a lot. And, do you remember those shop owners in the market in Morocco? They interacted with their customers a lot. They spent a lot of time drinking tea with customers to get to know them better.

Student 1: She also talks a lot about planning, so she must think that's really important. Remember, we had a whole class about business plans. I think we need to study the parts of a business plan.

Student 2: Oh, no—she could ask us to write a business plan!

Student 1: Well, the test is only an hour, so that's not enough time for that.

Student 3: Yeah, you're right.

Student 2: So, what do you think? Let's make a list of all the businesses we studied and the reasons they were successful.

Student 1: Good idea! First, we heard about that competition in Egypt. . . .

Pronunciation

Track 28   Thought Groups   Page 197

Our neighbor next door has a big brown dog.
After my class I'm going grocery shopping.
Finally after an hour the bus arrived.
On Sundays we usually go hiking in the park near our house.

Track 29   A.   Page 197

1. My oldest friend has been living in my neighborhood for 15 years.
2. Josh and I are going home after lunch.
3. She started a business last year when she graduated from technical college.
4. You have to speak in English for five minutes to pass the test.
5. There's a beautiful red bird singing in the tree.
6. There's an article in the newspaper about the 16-year-old girl in Malaysia.
7. Her experiences can teach us a lot about business success.
8. She might study business when she goes to college.

Video Scripts

Unit 1: Bee Therapy

Narrator:
Today in parts of Asia, people from all walks of life are choosing to be stung by bees—often dozens of times in one sitting. Hso-rong Chen is battling multiple sclerosis, a disease which slowly causes the body's nerves to deteriorate.

Hso-rong Chen, Patient:
For six months I was bedridden. I could not move. I would have symptoms of tingling and numbness in my hands. It was excruciating pain.

Narrator:
Then Hso-rong heard about bee-sting therapy. For help, she turned to Mr. Cheng-yi Chen, Bee-Sting Therapy Master—a trained master who has practiced bee-sting therapy for 12 years. Every week, Mr. Chen and his assistants treat 200 patients and sacrifice 6000 honeybees. The results, he says, can be astounding.

Mr. Cheng-yi Chen, Bee-Sting Therapy Master:
After 600 bees, you will look five years younger than your contemporaries.

Narrator:
But can bee stings really help Hso-rong fight multiple sclerosis? She began an intensive course of therapy, receiving over 200 stings a week for months on end. Honeybees only sting once, and they die soon after. But even separated from the bee, the stinger continues to inject venom into its victim. The body responds with a flood of histamines and white blood cells. And soon the area becomes hot, red, swollen, and itchy.

Hso-rong Chen:
He gives me one sting. I don't even have time to feel the pain before he stings me again. And the pain lasts for one hour.

Narrator:
Many think it is based on the 5000-year-old practice of acupuncture—a proven treatment for pain. Although today Mr. Chen sees bee acupuncture as a labor of love, even he once considered it taboo. In fact, like most of us, he was afraid of bees. 30 years ago, Mr. Chen was an executive for a textiles company. Then his wife began to suffer from arthritic pains so severe she couldn't cook or even stand up straight. Western medicines didn't do much good. But when she told her husband she wanted to get stung by bees, he thought the idea was ridiculous.

Mr. Cheng-yi Chen:
Naturally, as an educated man, I was against it. We just did not understand bees.

Narrator:
But Mr. Chen completely changed his mind when he saw his wife's sudden improvement.

Mr. Cheng-yi Chen:
After three months, her red blood cell count increased. Her headache disappeared. I was so surprised, I decided to dive into this mysterious treatment and collect all the information that I could.

Narrator:
Mr. Chen vowed to devote his life to bringing bee-sting therapy to others. After six months of bee-sting therapy, Hso-rong Chen has seen a dramatic change. She insists the therapy has relieved her multiple sclerosis and given her a new lease on life. While most Western-trained doctors would likely say her illness is in remission, Hso-rong is convinced the stings have helped her walk again. It will take years of study before we'll know whether bee stings can relieve arthritis, or multiple sclerosis, or even the common cold. But whether Hso-rong's recovery is in her head or her hands and feet, for the first time in more than a year she feels she can resume living. A therapy most of us would find taboo is allowing her to face the future with renewed hope.

Unit 2: Alternative Energy

Narrator:
The world seems to have an insatiable appetite for oil, electricity, and natural gas. But now, due to energy costs and global warming, scientists are looking to the wind, sun, and agricultural products to power our future. According to some researchers, wind power is becoming a more viable energy source.

Sandy Butterfield, Researcher:
I think the past perception was that wind energy was nice, but not a real solution. That perception is changing. I see wind energy getting more and more competitive.

Narrator:
At the National Renewable Energy Laboratory in Golden, Colorado, discovering alternative power sources that are competitive with fossil fuels has been a mission of scientists since the U.S. energy crisis of the 1970s. Scientists here also create solar cells that are far more efficient than those currently available to the public. They believe that the market for this technology is about to increase significantly.

John Brenner, National Renewable Energy Laboratory:
Recent polls have shown that about 75 percent of the population would favor the use of solar power, clean power, and would like to see more of it happening.

Narrator:
Solar power has been around for centuries, but while the public says they like the idea of harnessing solar power and incorporating it into their daily lives, the reality for many seems to be that it's something reserved for the future, not now.

Larry Kazmerski, Researcher:
Sometimes, you know, you worry that they think that this is only a fringe, but it's not. Photovoltaic, solar electricity is becoming a technology that is becoming cost-effective for us as consumers in the United States.

Narrator:
In many people's opinions, it often takes a crisis for things to change.

Larry Kazmerski:
When your electricity doesn't come on in California, you start looking very, very quickly!

Narrator:
For some, home use of solar power is now becoming more than just an abstract idea. When Jonathon Sawyer's solar electric system was first installed, it was believed to be the largest residential solar system in the United States. This is likely due to the fact that solar power had not been widely promoted at the time. It's so efficient that he actually sells electricity back to his local power company.

Jonathon Sawyer, Solar Homeowner:
I also feel good because I've always been committed about the environment and doing something, and we have to start as individuals to do things.

Narrator:
But individuals can only do so much. Researchers claim that for renewable energy to truly make a difference, it must be used on a large scale.

Pat Woodard, Reporter
This is a solar concentrator. The mirrors focus the sun's rays into a narrow beam which turns an engine and provides electricity. Tough to get in the backyard? Sure. But a power company could probably find a place for it.

Narrator:
The United States and other countries often lacked a great sense of urgency to find energy alternatives. For decades, gasoline prices had been kept low with government subsidies so people continued driving large cars—usually alone. Nowadays, gasoline costs are higher, which has enhanced the need to find something else to fuel all those vehicles.

John Sheehan, Alternative Fuel Researcher:
What's in there now is material that looks like straw, or . . . It's actually the material that farmers leave sitting on the ground after they go through and they harvest corn. We're trying to get farmers to collect this material so that we can run it through a conversion technology to make new liquid fuels.

Narrator:
Since the energy crisis of the 1970s, many farmers have been turning food into fuel by using grains like corn to create ethanol. But recently, some of the emphasis on making fuel has been moving away from the grain itself—to the stalks and stubble left on the ground after the harvest.

John Sheehan:
The cellulose that's in here—that actually is made up of sugars—is something that they can turn into ethanol in the same way that they're currently taking their corn grain and having it turned into fuel-grade ethanol.

Narrator:
The National Renewable Energy Laboratory has a manufacturing area that is capable of converting harvest leftovers—and just about anything else—into fuel.

Pat Woodard:
What are some of these other materials here? What else we got?

John Sheehan:
Some of these, like this for example, is a wood material.

Narrator:
Proving that sustainable energy technology is actually viable remains a struggle, at least in the United States. Wind turbines, which were pioneered in the United States, are now being used by several countries in Europe to supply meaningful amounts of power.

Sandy Butterfield:
The cost of energy in the United States is so low compared to Europe that our industry has had a harder time competing with fossil fuels.

Narrator:
The cost of fuel in many countries has increased significantly over the past few years. While it has caused hardship for many, this cost increase may also increase the urgency to find reliable fossil fuel alternatives and thereby reduce the greenhouse gases that cause global warming. The time for alternative energy may have arrived—and for those who use it, the future may be now.

Unit 3: The Gauchos of Argentina

Narrator:
In the country of Argentina, cowboy life has scarcely changed over the past three centuries. The *gaucho* is a hero here; for most people, he is a legendary figure that is larger than life. But in the far reaches of the country, there are still men for whom the *gaucho* is more than a legend. For them, it is their life; they are the *gauchos* of Argentina. The cowboy life of the *gaucho* came to Argentina from Spanish culture. It created a unique type of men who were as hardy and self-reliant as the animals for which they cared. The word "gaucho" means "outcast," or one who doesn't belong to a specific society or group. There are as many kinds of *gauchos* as there are varied terrains in Argentina. There are *gauchos* on the soft, flat pampas

of Corrientes, on the windswept plains of Patagonia, and in the wooded hills of Salta. Don José Ansola, a 76-year-old horseman, seems to be the "classic *gaucho*," and one who treasures his residence in a remote region of Corrientes. He believes solitude helps to keep *gaucho* life in its purest form.

Don José Ansola, Corrientes *Gaucho*:
If I couldn't live in the *campo*, the countryside—an unthinkable thought—I don't know what I'd do.

Narrator:
According to Don José, he would rather live in a poor little house in the country than in a palace in the city. Don José's 154-square-mile ranch in Corrientes is far from everything, so Don José depends entirely on his horses to travel. As a result, he and his three sons spend much of their time finding and catching the wild horses that run free in the countryside. The horses must then be "broken" so that they'll allow people to ride them.

Don José Ansola:
Breaking a horse is a slow process, taking more than a year. This is something the horse learns to put up with.

Narrator:
The *gaucho* explains that the horse must adjust to using a saddle and reins so the riders aren't thrown off later. The treatment seems cruel, but according to Don José, it's actually not. The training, he says, often seems harsher than it is.

Don José Ansola:
We love our horses, and in the end, they love us in return. This is the traditional way of training a horse in Argentina—the *gaucho* way.

Narrator:
Being a *gaucho*, though, is more than a life of solitude and caring for horses and cattle. The *gaucho* way of life has its own strict code of ethics.

Hospitality and respect for others are as much a part of this lifestyle as the art of breaking horses. Argentina is nearly the last place where this code of ethics and the demanding lifestyle of the *gaucho* still exist. The country is home to nearly 150,000 *gauchos,* who are very much a part of the national identity. There are *gauchos* in all parts of the country, even more than 1200 miles south of Buenos Aires, on the edge of Antarctica in Patagonia. The harsh terrain of this region has its own type of *gaucho* as well. Here, the *gauchos* raise sheep, not cattle, and even more surprisingly, many speak English. Many of the ancestors of Patagonian *gauchos* were immigrants from Scotland. Several of these settlers came to the area during the 19th century, including the ancestors of Eduardo Halliday and his father, Jimmy. These two *gauchos* run a ranch in Patagonia, and for them, this strange terrain seems like the perfect place to live.

The Hallidays enjoy living in the region for a number of reasons. For Jimmy, the most refreshing aspect about living in Patagonia is that there's space everywhere so he can see far in all directions. The land is also rich, he says, and produces everything that he and his family need. Life on the plains of Patagonia is difficult, even harsh, but the *gauchos* here have learned how to adjust and succeed. Eduardo has lived his entire life on the family ranch and has learned the traditional ways from his father. The goal of every *gaucho* is self-reliance, and these *gauchos* of Patagonia are no different. Because the ranch is so remote, father and son have to utilize everything they have available. This also means they don't abandon anything quickly and often use and reuse everything they have, including their bags and their boots. After all, it's a long way to go to buy new ones. *Gauchos* are experts at adjusting to their surroundings. Here, they've learned to use a local weapon called a *boleadora*. Made of leather and small stones, *boleadoras* are still used to hunt *rhea*. Pursuing the small, flightless birds is no problem, but hitting them can be tough. As the *gauchos* fly like the wind along the plains on their strong horses, the *rheas* run swiftly ahead of them. It's an exciting chase, but the *rheas* get away—this time. About 1800 miles north of Patagonia is the region of Salta. Here the stony hills and rough terrain have produced yet a different kind of *gaucho*. The *gauchos* here were once fierce soldiers for Argentina, and they won recognition and respect in the Argentine war of independence from Spain. They're famous for their huge leather chaps and red ponchos, and often celebrate their proud traditions in an annual parade. One of the best horsemen in the area is Rudecindo Campos. Rudecindo loves being a *gaucho* and says that it's the life he's always wanted.

Rudecindo Campos, Salta *Gaucho*:
In life there are all kinds of people: engineers, doctors, and *gauchos*. I knew I had to choose one or the other. I have always had a *gaucho* soul, and I like being a *gaucho*.

Narrator:
However, choosing the life of a *gaucho* means more than just working with horses. Just as it is in Corrientes, a strict code of ethics and principles is essential to the *gaucho* lifestyle in Salta as well.

Don Coco Campos, Rudecindo's Father:
It's not only knowing how to catch an animal with a rope, use a saddle, or ride a horse. It's also about being good and kind. When you ask a *gaucho* a favor, he must not refuse. He does it.

Narrator:
At times, it's difficult to make enough money working as a *gaucho*. In order to survive, Rudecindo must work at a part-time job so he can continue training horses. He specializes in training a strong little horse from the area called a *criollo*. It's one of the few animals that can

round up cattle in this rough terrain covered with thorns. To protect themselves from the environment, horse and rider rely on their special leather chaps. The thick leather protects the pair from injuries as they round up the last of the cattle. In Salta, each time the *gauchos* successfully return the cattle safely back to the ranch, there's a lively *fiesta,* a celebration in which women have always had an important role. Rudecindo's wife, who comes from the city, talks about life on the ranch.

Rudecindo's Wife:
It's very difficult to adapt to the slower pace of the *campo.* In the city, you live faster, and you are less attentive to nature. We've lost that in the city. We've lost some of our humanity, which my husband hasn't lost. He's not caught up in the trivia of everyday life. You can really get consumed by small things, and you forget what's important.

Rudecindo Campos:
If I go into town for two weeks, I can't wait to get home to the horses, to the smell of the countryside, and the wet earth after a rain. I love this life.

Narrator:
In the end, the story of today's *gaucho* may be one of adaptation—to climate, to landscape, and to traditional ways of life that sustain them.

Don José Ansola:
For Argentina, it's very important for people to treasure this proud and honorable legacy. We must be sure that whatever else happens to us, we never lose our heritage, our *gaucho* way of life.

Narrator:
Don José is not alone in his dream. The proud and self-reliant *gauchos* of Corrientes, Patagonia, and Salta are all helping to retain the traditional lifestyle of the *gauchos* of Argentina.

Unit 4: More Water for India

Narrator:
New Delhi is a large city in northern India. The air here can be so dirty that it's sometimes difficult to see the city. The water supply doesn't look much better.

The Yamuna River runs through the city. Every day, 50 million gallons of chemicals are put into the river. This river is the city's main source of drinking water. The 14 million people in and around New Delhi must get their water from community water trucks. These trucks distribute water to the places where people live. Sometimes there's enough water for everyone, and sometimes there isn't. The people of New Delhi require about one billion gallons of water a day. They only receive about 25 percent of that. In the rich parts of the city, you'll find busy shopping centers, well-dressed shoppers, and expensive restaurants. But their water still comes on trucks. Outside of Delhi, in the region of Rajasthan, getting water is even harder. The temperatures frequently reach 120 degrees Fahrenheit or 50 degrees Celsius. People have to walk for miles to get water from a well. Then they often have to drink next to their animals. Once a year, there is a lot of rain, during a time called the monsoon season. But people need water all year. What can India do to solve its water problems? Some in the government says the answer is to build more big dams. But many people disagree with that idea. They think that India's dams have made the water problem worse by drying up rivers and wells.

Rajendra Singh, Environmentalist:
Thousands of millions of rupees have already been invested in water policy and big dams. How do you explain villages with no water? Who is responsible for all this? Well, the blame lies on the very system which advocates the construction of bigger dams.

Narrator:
A man named Rajendra Singh has a different idea to solve the problem. He started an organization that works with people in the villages to make clean water easily available. He teaches them to build very small dams to store water and change the land. People in the Alwar region decided to try Singh's idea. They began collecting stone and rock and made small earthen dams. They then made small holes near them and covered them with stone, earth, and clay. This stopped rainwater from running off and raised the level of the water under the ground. Every time it rained, the groundwater level got higher. The people made wells to bring water to their farms, and soon, water reached every part of the village. Today, a village that was dry and lifeless is green and healthy. Because of two small earthen dams, farmers who couldn't grow enough food for their families can now produce food for them. And the idea has spread. . . .

Rosda Rajasthan, Villager:
We're building water reservoirs and dams to save rain water. We want our village, Rosda, to be green and prosperous like Neemie.

Narrator:
Now more than 4000 small earthen dams collect rainwater across western India. They provide water for more than 800 communities. Small dams like these aren't practical for the people of New Delhi. They couldn't provide enough water. Experts say that in New Delhi, water conservation and new water supplies could make life better for about 10 years. But the work of Rajendra Singh in Alwar shows that change is possible. Now, the people there don't have to walk many miles for water. Clean, fresh water is always close by. His success shows that the people in different places need to find the solution that is right for them.

Unit 5: Memory Man

Narrator:
Gianni Golfera is in front of a group of people. He's blindfolded, but he can still show them something that's amazing. The young Italian man calls it "the art of memory." First, the people randomly choose 60 numbers. After that, a helper reads the numbers to Gianni. Then Gianni repeats the numbers in the correct order from memory. First, in the order he heard them. Then again—backwards!

Gianni Golfera:
It's a kind of memory that is connected to what I see. It means that every idea I learn, everything I read, becomes a part of me. Normally, a person who doesn't have this gift and who hasn't studied memory tends to just forget things. Even an entire book. Not me.

Narrator:
Gianni has a special kind of memory. He has memorized more than 250 books. He also says that he can remember every detail of every day of his life—from the time he was less than one year old! Memory is very difficult to understand, and scientists don't really know how it works. The Golfera family genes may hold important information about Gianni's memory. Neurobiologist Dr. Antonio Malgaroli plans to compare the Golfera family's genes with the genes of more forgetful families.

Dr. Antonio Malgaroli, Neurobiologist:
The crucial question is to understand which is the contribution from heredity, and which is the contribution that comes from the environment.

Narrator:
When we process new information, such as reading a book or newspaper, it goes into our brains through the hippocampus. There, it's coded as memory. But how is memory coded? Where is it stored? Why is it stored there? Nobody knows. Nobody knows why some people lose their memories, or why so few people, like Gianni, never forget things. Researchers are now studying how memory and learning change the brain. They're also trying to match those changes to specific genes. Some research shows that a great memory may not depend on the right DNA.

Dr. Antonio Malgaroli:
If you really need to use your brain capacity to store some kind of information, you have this ability. It's just a matter of exercise.

Narrator:
The same idea is true for Gianni. His genes are only part of the story. Since the age of 11, he's been training his brain to remember. He practices continuously to improve the power of his memory. He has even memorized a whole series of historical books. For Gianni, improving his memory has become almost like a full-time job.

Dr. Antonio Malgaroli:
Golfera has an extraordinary ability. The question is . . . how much it's really because of the Golfera family genes and how much comes from his sort of maniac type of activity?

Narrator:
Gianni's life is not all about science, though. He has a relatively normal life. He has a dog and a girlfriend. He likes to take time away from work. In other words, he's just like other people, and that's part of what's so interesting. His genes are partly responsible for his great memory. However, researchers think it's mainly because of his very hard work, and Gianni agrees. He even offers proof. He holds classes to teach people how to improve their memories. His system involves organization and hard work—basically learning how to "remember to remember."

Gianni Golfera:
I think the only problem with memory is getting the correct order. There's a lot of brain space, so I think there are no limits.

Narrator:
If there is a memory gene, Gianni Golfera probably has it. But the success of "The Memory Man" may be more about determination than DNA. Gianni's practice and hard work are making his memory even better. He might just be showing scientists that a great memory can be made, and not just born!

Unit 6: The Food and Culture of Oaxaca

Narrator:
Let's travel to Mexico now, to the historic state of Oaxaca. It's a place that's famous for its traditions—and its food. If you feel cold in winter, you can warm up in Oaxaca by enjoying its spicy chilies, its beautiful dances, and its lovely streets and buildings. When you come to Oaxaca, beautiful colors and wonderful smells are all around you. Oaxaca is one of the poorest states in Mexico, but it's rich in culture. And Oaxacan food is famous around the world.

Susana Trilling, Cooking Instructor:
It's one of the best foods—it's very complex.

Narrator:
Susana Trilling loves the chilies in Oaxacan food. She moved here 14 years ago to start her own cooking school. Many foreigners have come to learn how to make real Oaxacan mole and other dishes. Susana's students heard about Oaxacan food in their own countries. And they come here wanting to learn more. People stay in Oaxaca and take cooking classes at the

school. Oaxacan food developed a long time before people came from Europe to America. Tradition is keeping this food alive, and Susana thinks Oaxacan food is as interesting and difficult to make as Thai food, or French food. It uses many different ingredients. The first step in cooking Oaxacan food is making a sauce called *mole*. *Mole* is made from chili peppers, spices, and various other ingredients. *Mole* is standard in many different Oaxacan dishes. People serve it with chicken and meat, and everything else. But Oaxacan culture is more than just food. The state is also famous for its dances. This dance is centuries old. It's called the *Guelagetza*. It tells about the culture, history, and music of the Oaxacan people. The buildings in the city are large and beautiful. Many of them are Mexican national treasures. This building is 500 years old, with fountains, gardens, and archways. In the past, it was a government building. Today, it's a luxury hotel. Oaxacan people say that a healthy person is happy and loves to work and eat. After a short visit to Oaxaca, you can see that that tradition is still true.

Unit 7: Volcano Trek

Narrator:
Millions of years ago, man's earliest ancestors lived in a far region of Ethiopia. In this area, hot lava has erupted from the Erta Ale volcano for about 100 years. The temperature of this lava is more than 2000 degrees Fahrenheit. Now, a team of explorers is going to see Erta Ale for themselves. They want to learn more about the volcano. It's not an easy trek, and the team has to use camels. They finally reach the crater. Franck Tessier and Irene Margaritis are geologists and professors at the University of Nice. They've traveled halfway around the world to see Erta Ale. Deep in the crater, they see the black lava lake.

Professor Irene Margaritis:
It is quite exciting. I want to see it now.

Narrator:
Erta Ale is in the Afar area of Ethiopia. The Afar triangle is in an area where three continental plates meet. These plates move farther apart every year. The Erta Ale volcano has the oldest lava lake in the world. The lake is also one of the lowest points on Earth. At Erta Ale, geologists study how the world started millions of years ago. Red hot lava comes out from deep in the earth. This lava forms Erta Ale's lava lake. As the lava cools down, it becomes hard and black. Hot magma breaks through this covering as the volcano erupts. The geologists stand at the top of the active volcano and wait at the side of the crater. It's not easy to be there; there is a strong smell of sulfur. Even in the early morning, it's very, very hot. Then the group goes down into the crater. Professor Tessier wants to collect samples of the red-hot lava. It's two o'clock in the morning before they return. They're very tired and, as Professor Margaritis says . . .

Irene Margaritis:
Very hot!

Professor Franck Tessier:
I think this is fresh lava.

Narrator:
The pieces didn't come directly from the lava lake. However, the team decides they're fresh enough. The team will now go back to analyze the samples. As professors, they want to learn new information that they can teach to others. However as geologists, they want to know what the lava of Erta Ale may teach them about how the world began millions of years ago.

Unit 8: The Lost City of Machu Picchu

Narrator:
This beautiful, quiet place is covered in sunshine and has mountains all around it. Its name is Machu Picchu. It's sometimes called the Lost City of the Incas, and it's nearly 8000 feet up in the Andes.

Julio, Tour Guide:
It's a magic attraction that you can feel here. It's known all over the world that Machu Picchu is one of the magnetic centers of the ancient world.

Narrator:
Machu Picchu is more than 500 years old. Today, it's a favorite place for visitors from all over the world. Even in the rain and fog, it's wonderful to walk through the ruins. When the Inca civilization ended, few people knew Machu Picchu existed. For a long time, it was lost to the outside world. Then, in 1911, an explorer named Hiram Bingham found it again. At first, very few people visited Machu Picchu. But now, hundreds of tourists come here every day. They walk up the steps of the ancient city and climb over the ruins. Machu Picchu is no longer quiet. It's full of the sounds of tourists. Some people in Peru hope that more tourists will come here. They think it will mean more business and money for the country. However, some conservationists worry that more visitors won't be good for Machu Picchu. They say that tourism might not be good for the environment. Jose, a local hotel owner, says Machu Picchu and Peru can take a few more visitors.

Jose, Hotel Owner:
Why not be like the rest of the world? Why not expose and show Machu Picchu to the rest of the world? It's such a wonderful place, why keep it to a few?

Narrator:
The truth is that parts of Peru are very poor, and tourists bring money to these communities. Aguas Calientes is a town that grew suddenly near an area where visitors

get on buses to get to the summit of Machu Picchu. The people here live completely on money from tourism. The town is just a group of stalls where local people sell art and things they have made to visitors. The Lost City is no longer lost. Tourists have found it. The modern world is coming closer to this ancient world every day. Time may be running out for the Lost City of the Incas. More and more people are discovering it. In the end, it may be the modern world that forever changes this ancient city.

Unit 9: A Disappearing World

Narrator:
It's September in the Congo . . . just north of the equator. An expedition unlike any other is beginning. A team of scientists and researchers is traveling nearly 1200 miles, or 2000 kilometers, through a rainforest that covers almost 58,000 square miles, or 150,000 square kilometers. Their aim is to make a scientific record of a world that could be disappearing from Earth: the Congo Basin. Dr. Michael Fay is a scientist from the Wildlife Conservation Society. He's leading the expedition he calls "The Megatransect," or "The Big Crossing." According to Fay, if they don't document the wildlife here now, there may never be another chance to do it!

Dr. Michael Fay, Wildlife Conservation Society:
What I'm trying to do, in a desperate way, is to show the world that we're just about to lose the last little gem in the African continent. And if we don't do something now . . . if we don't do it today, we can forget about it.

Narrator:
The Congo Basin contains almost one quarter of the world's rainforests. It may have up to half of all of the wild plants and animals found in all of Africa. Fay's plan is to collect and record data on almost every part of the rainforest. He wants to document the trees, the plants, and the animals that he sees there. It's a job that's going to take time. After eight months of traveling, the team is now in Gabon. Their next challenge is to reach a group of strange hills that are made of stone, and which rise far above the forest floor. At last, the men reach the hills and begin to walk up. Suddenly, they realize that they're finally above the tops of the trees.

Michael Fay:
We can see a long way here, you know . . . 70 or 80 kilometers in every direction. We can see 360 degrees around. There are no humans. There's not a single village, there's not a single road. It's an amazing place.

Narrator:
The team continues. They can hear their next challenge before they reach it. Rapids!

Michael Fay:
OK, wow.

Narrator:
The Kongou Chutes are an important part of the landscape that the team wants to protect. This land of fast water and old forests is in danger because of logging. Right now, the team has a more immediate problem. They must cross the dangerous river here. It's only a few hundred meters wide, but the team must use guide ropes, stepping stones, and everything they know to get across. It takes a full day . . . and there's still a long way to go! After more than a year, the team finally reaches the end of their travels.

Michael Fay:
We'd been walking in the woods in our own little world for 15 months and now it was over. I was overwhelmed.

Narrator:
Dr. Fay's expedition walked through some of the wildest lands of Africa. They documented as many of the things they found as possible. And they did it all in an attempt to save a disappearing world.

Unit 10: Making a Deal in Fes

Narrator:
The *souk* in the city of Fes is Morocco's oldest market. In one of its small stalls, a craftsman is making patterns on a metal tabletop. But all around him, people are making deals. This is business, Moroccan-style. Sales in the *souk* happen face-to-face; it's very personal and very busy! The vendors have everything a shopper could want. Sandals are next to fish bowls, and nearby, birds in cages watch the scene. One vendor sells kaftans, others sell slippers or jewelry. Across the alley, a man sells dates and apricots to hungry shoppers. In the *souk,* there really is something for everyone. And in the city of Fes, a certain kind of small, red hat is very easy to find. The *fez* was created here and named after the city. A visit to the *souk* is a lesson in Moroccan bargaining culture. For visitors, the question is not *What should I buy?*, but *How should I buy it?*. That's where they get a real education in making a deal.

Vincent, Dutch Tourist:
You have to start yourself at one third or something, and then you bargain up to 50 percent.

Consuela, Dutch Tourist:
Yeah, and they go down twice as hard as we go up with the price. So, then you get it at half the price they say at first.

Vincent:
But it's really a game. The Moroccans are very good at bargaining, and they say they are the best in the world.

Ahmed, Tour Guide:
You know, here in Moroccan culture, for everything . . . you should bargain. We don't have really a fixed price.

Narrator:
In the *souk,* shopping is an exercise in bargaining. Here, it's the natural thing to do, and just about everyone does it. However, visitors who want to practice making a deal here had better be careful! They ought to know a few things first—beginners at bargaining pay more. How much more?

Ahmed:
Sometimes 20, 30 percent more . . . than the price that the Moroccan people pay. So you should always . . . for example, if he charges you 1000 dirham, you give him 600 dirham, then you go up, he go down, and then you can arrange between you.

Narrator:
Vendors aren't trying to cheat customers. It's like a test to find out who's the best bargainer.

Mohcine, Jewelry Vendor:
Some customers pay more than another one . . . we find customers . . . more easy . . . they don't bargain too much.

Narrator:
The real test for any bargainer is the carpet shop. This is where the sellers really pressure customers to buy something.

Chakib, Carpet Vendor:
Excuse me, you want to buy camel for the price of donkey? Impossible. No, that's too low, believe me, that's too low.

Chris, English Tourist:
Once you end up in a shop, you sit there drinking tea, and you say, "I don't want to buy anything." But then it's like,

"Well, just offer a price . . . offer a price. 500? What's your best price?" And you're like, "We don't want to buy it." And they're like, "OK, 300!"

Narrator:
But it's all part of the game.

Chakib:
Well, we ask a little bit high price because everyone comes with an intention to bargain. They know that in Morocco they bargain a lot, so of course we leave a step to make discounts and haggling the price.

Narrator:
Some shoppers enjoy the challenge, too.

Gonnie, Carpet Shopper:
The secret is looking very carefully at how they do it. And watch them, how they move . . . and then go step-by-step and see where you end.

Narrator:
There is one thing that all tourists should watch out for—they shouldn't buy too much!

Bo, Dutch Tourist:
The thing is, they make it so cheap for you! They start up so high, and at the end it sounds so cheap. It's only one-sixth of the price, or one-eighth of the price. Well, for this money, I can't leave it!

Narrator:
For some visitors to Fes, it may be difficult to leave without buying more than they planned. One thing here is certain—at the *souk,* everyone can make a deal!

DATE DUE